HARPSICHORD MUSIC

RECENT RESEARCHES IN THE MUSIC OF THE BAROQUE ERA

Robert L. Marshall, general editor

A-R Editions, Inc., publishes six quarterly series—

Recent Researches in the Music of the Middle Ages and Early Renaissance
Margaret Bent, general editor

Recent Researches in the Music of the Renaissance
James Haar, general editor

Recent Researches in the Music of the Baroque Era
Robert L. Marshall, general editor

Recent Researches in the Music of the Classical Era
Eugene K. Wolf, general editor

Recent Researches in the Music of the Nineteenth and Early Twentieth Centuries
Rufus Hallmark, general editor

Recent Researches in American Music
H. Wiley Hitchcock, general editor—

which make public music that is being brought to light
in the course of current musicological research.

Each volume in the *Recent Researches* is devoted
to works by a single composer or to a single genre of composition,
chosen because of its potential interest to scholars and performers,
and prepared for publication according to the standards that govern
the making of all reliable historical editions.

Subscribers to this series, as well as patrons of subscribing institutions,
are invited to apply for information about the "Copyright-Sharing Policy"
of A-R Editions, Inc., under which the contents of this volume
may be reproduced free of charge for study or performance.

Correspondence should be addressed:

A-R EDITIONS, INC.
315 West Gorham Street
Madison, Wisconsin 53703

RECENT RESEARCHES IN THE MUSIC OF THE BAROQUE ERA • VOLUME LVI

Giovanni Battista Draghi

HARPSICHORD MUSIC

Edited by Robert Klakowich

A-R EDITIONS, INC. • MADISON

Library of Congress Cataloging-in-Publication Data

Draghi, Giovanni Battista, ca. 1640–1708.
  Harpsichord music.

  (Recent researches in the music of the Baroque Era,
ISSN 0484–0828 ; v. 56)
  Edited from Draghi's Six select suites of lessons for
the harpsichord (London : Walsh, 1707?) and several mss.
  Includes bibliographical references.
  1. Harpsichord Music. I. Title. II. Series.
M2.R238   vol. 56   [M22]   86–754056
ISBN 0–89579–216–8

Contents

Preface

Among the Italian musicians serving the English royal household after the Restoration, Giovanni Battista Draghi enjoyed a distinguished career of some forty years. Contemporary accounts point out that Draghi was a keyboard player of the highest order, and his works for harpsichord fit stylistically into the English mainstream represented by Locke, Blow, and Purcell. Unlike those renowned composers, Draghi's principal output is for the keyboard, and the music reflects a keen sensitivity to the sonorous possibilities of the harpsichord. His eighty-five surviving harpsichord pieces, collected from printed and manuscript sources, appear here for the first time in a modern edition.

The Composer

Little is known of the life of Draghi prior to his association with the court of Charles II, and nothing of his Italian origins. We may entertain the possibility that he was a brother of Antonio Draghi (b. 1634 or 1635), who also spent most of his life in a foreign country (as Kapellmeister to Leopold I in Vienna). Antonio Draghi was born in Rimini and began his career in Vienna in 1658. Assuming that Giovanni Battista did not emigrate to England until after the Restoration (after 1660), one can surmise that he was younger than Antonio—hence, Rimini ca. 1640 is usually suggested as the place and date of his birth.[1]

The earliest mention of him is this entry for 12 February 1667, by the famous diarist Samuel Pepys:

> The Italian Signor Baptista . . . hath composed a play in Italian for the Opera, which T. Killigrew do intend to have up; and here he did sing one of the acts. He himself is the poet as well as the musician, which is very much, and did sing the whole from the words, without any music prickt, and played all along on a harpsicon most admirably, and the composition most excellent. . . . He pretends not to voice, though it be good, but not excellent. . . . My great wonder is, how that man do keep in memory so perfectly the musique of the whole act, both for the voice and the instrument too.

The opera in question, along with any record of its performance, seems to have vanished without a trace, but Draghi's fortunes did not rise or fall with Charles II's futile attempts to plant Italian opera in English soil. "Mr. Baptist," as Draghi was most commonly called in England, went on to become a favored musician at the courts of successive English monarchs until his death in 1708.

We cannot be certain that Draghi yet held an official position in the royal court in 1667. We do know that in 1673 he became principal organist to the queen consort Catherine of Braganza at Somerset House. His predecessor was Matthew Locke, who nevertheless remained there in semi-retirement until his death four years later.

Not noted for his congeniality towards foreign musicians, Locke might have accepted this situation in something less than agreeable terms. Roger North had this comment:

> Mr Lock was organist of Somerset House, much the best master in his time. . . . But Sigr Babtista Draghe was made cheif [sic] organist, and had the great organ, but Lock was not put out, having a chamber organ that stood by, which he accompanied with; so just are Kings and Queens sometimes.[2]

Draghi's annual salary as organist in 1677–78 was £150.[3] (Locke was paid £100 six years earlier.[4]) In the meantime both composers had contributed music to *Psyche*, and according to Shadwell's 1675 preface of the libretto, Draghi now held the important position of Master of the Italian Music to the King.

The events of the Popish Plot of 1678, among which five prominent Catholic lords and the confessor to the Duchess of York were sent to the Tower, apparently prompted Draghi to sign a petition of appeal, together with three of the king's other Italian musicians who may have feared deportation because of Catholic sympathies. The substance of the petition, which was referred to the Treasury on 18 November 1679, was that the musicians had left the service of foreign princes at the king's request, and that they were serving him faithfully despite the fact that their salaries were four years in arrears.[5] Whatever the outcome of this appeal, Draghi remained in England and retained his royal posts.

In 1684 Draghi found himself a participant in a competition involving the building of the new organ in the Temple Church. The two candidates were the rival builders Bernard Schmidt, who came to be known as Father Smith, and Renatus Harris. Each had an instrument erected in a different part of the church, and Thomas Tudway, the well-known church music anthologist, wrote a letter to his son containing a vivid account of how the contest was staged:

> Dr Blow and Mr Purcell, who was then in his prime, shewed and played Father Smith's organ on appointed days to a numerous audience. . . . Mr Harris brought [Draghi], organist to Queen Catherine, a very eminent master, to touch his organ . . . they thus continued vying with one another near a twelvemonth.[6]

It was Smith's organ that eventually stayed in the church, although Harris went on to become one of London's most successful organ builders.

By the 1680s Draghi's fame as a performer and composer must already have been considerable, to judge from these anecdotes in the diary of John Evelyn:

> I din'd at my Lord Falklands, Treasurer of the Navy, where after dinner we had rare Musique, there being amongst others Signor Pietro Reggio and Signor Jo Battist

bothe famous, the one for his Voice, and the other for his playing on the Harpsichord, few if any in Europe exceeding him. (25 July 1684)

I was invited to my Lord Arundel of Wardour, where after dinner . . . Mr. Pordage entertained us with his voice, that excellent and stupendous artist Signor John Baptist playing to it on the harpsichord. (28 January 1685)

For St. Cecilia's Day, 1687, Draghi was chosen to set Dryden's ode "From harmony, from heavenly harmony." Several of the plays produced at Dorset Garden Theatre and Lincoln's Inn Fields from 1682 to 1696 contained his music, and he contributed abundantly to song collections of the time published by the Playfords and others.

After the death of Charles II, Draghi evidently stayed on at Somerset House with the queen dowager, and in 1688 he became organist of the Chapel Royal under James II. At some point, he also was charged with the musical instruction of the princesses Mary and Anne (later Queen Mary and Queen Anne).[7] When Catherine departed London in 1692 to return to her native Portugal, Draghi's position at court was maintained under William and Mary.

In 1695 an abortive attempt was made at founding a Royal Academy to provide instruction in several of the arts and sciences, including music. The name "Mr. Baptist" appears in an advertisement as one of the four teachers of organ and harpsichord.[8] Another name mentioned here is "Mr. Purcell," either Henry (who died on 21 November of that year) or his younger brother Daniel, who had just returned to London from Oxford.

Towards the end of his life, Draghi apparently became incapacitated by gout, and advertisements of concerts for his benefit appeared in the *London Gazette*, the *Post Boy*, and the *Post Man* between 1698 and 1701.[9] William III awarded him an annual pension in 1698, which was confirmed by Queen Anne on her succession in 1702. A document dated 28 July 1708 indicates that the queen granted £25 "to Sibilla Baptiste Draghi for the funeral of John Baptiste Draghi."[10]

Among Draghi's compositions his harpsichord pieces form the largest group, and they perhaps best represent his style. His most ambitious work is the ode for St. Cecilia's Day, "From harmony, from heavenly harmony" on a text by Dryden.[11] He also wrote over two dozen solo songs, some specifically for plays, as well as two solo cantatas on Italian texts and some music for instruments other than keyboard. Only his *Six Select Suites of Lessons* for harpsichord, and contributions to song anthologies, were published in his lifetime.[12]

The Harpsichord Music

What is immediately noticeable in Draghi's harpsichord music is the extent to which he absorbed the prevailing style of his adopted country. The eclectic nature of English keyboard music in the late seventeenth century, fusing traditional English characteristics with such continental ones as the French *style brisé*, is strongly reflected in Draghi's printed collection of 1707. This con-

tains groups of pieces in six different keys, each beginning with a prelude followed by binary dance types interspersed with airs, rondos, and the occasional character piece. Two examples of the latter are [12] The Hunting Tune and [36] The Dream, the titles of which suggest a relationship to typically English piece-types found as early as the Elizabethan period ("The Hunt's Up," "Giles Farnaby's Dream," etc.). In the manuscripts, there are also key-groups of similar make-up and style, as well as single pieces. Among the latter are two extended compositions found in the Washington manuscript (see below under Sources), namely [38] Toccata and [39] Trumpet. The Toccata is placed in the manuscript with a group of stylistically similar toccatas by Italian composers, including one by Bernardo Pasquini.[13] It was not a model prevalent in England at the time, although a few toccatas by Italian composers appeared in printed anthologies just after the turn of the century, and it is the only clear instance of Italianism in all of Draghi's harpsichord music. The Trumpet, again, is a work of distinctly English character, reflecting the English preoccupation with trumpet tunes such as those found in the music of many Restoration stage works.

The preludes of Draghi are short, through-composed pieces, most of which are characterized by technical features such as rapid arpeggios and scale passages ([1], [7], [13], [19], [32], [41], [74]). A couple of others ([25] and [65]) are more vocally conceived and exhibit a contemplative rather than brilliant mood. The two versions of the C-minor Prelude ([45]), found in two different sources, present an interesting illustration of both types. (Both versions are edited here.) The B-minor Prelude ([65]) employs partially unmeasured notation, as in French *préludes non mesurés*—this is the only English harpsichord prelude known to us with such notation.[14]

The almand is the dance type most often treated by Draghi; each suite in the edition has one, and several others exist in manuscript. The B-minor group has three ([66], [70], and [73]), the third untitled but reflecting the style and expressive quality of an almand. This last "almand" is remarkable for its extraordinary length (three repeated sections) and the powerfully grave quality it exhibits. Charles Babell, the scribe of British Library MS Add. 39569, reserved an uncharacteristic location for it at the end of the group. Rich textures, taking full advantage of the harpsichord's sonority, are present here, and this is a stylistic tendency that distinguishes Draghi's keyboard writing, particularly in almands, from Purcell's and Blow's.

The remaining dance types in Draghi's oeuvre may be more briefly described. The corants all have a distinctly French appearance and are, with one exception, in 3/2 ([63] is in 3/4). The sarabands vary in mood: some are lightly textured and unassuming in character, while others exude a serious tone. (Note the titles [4] The Complaint and [68] [Tombeau].) The designation "slow" in [22] and [47] may have served to indicate to the contemporary player that the quicker type of saraband, which frequently provided the finale to English keyboard suites at this time, was not intended here. The G-minor Saraband ([16]) is a gem of textural simplicity, its particular color created by the use of melodic double thirds throughout.

The titles "Aire" and "Arietta" are frequently found in the sources; these turn out to be in almost any time signature and may or may not be dance movements. The E-minor Aire of the edition ([5]) is called "Bouree" in the Washington manuscript. Some have folklike melodies, either of rather wistful quality ([30]) or rustic and forthright ([11], [34], and [49]). A small number of pieces are in rondo form ([24], [48], [71], and [72]), while a single ground survives ([84]), revealing a briskness that recalls Blow's well-known Mortlack's Ground.[15] Two pieces are simply titled "Tune" ([82] and [83]) and are possibly transcriptions of songs.

One striking hallmark of Draghi's style is his evident fondness for dissonant chords. Used effectively, they bring to mind sonorities later found in the sonatas of Domenico Scarlatti; see in particular [2] Allmand, m. 19; [12] The Hunting Tune, m. 15; [14] Allmand, m. 13; [47] Slow, m. 27; [66] [Allemande], m. 19; and [68] [Tombeau], m. 23. The notation of the chord in [21] Corrant, m. 10, showing ties for only the harmonic tones, may indicate that the non-harmonic tones here and elsewhere were intended to be played as acciaccaturas, to be released while the harmonic tones continued to sound. At other times, though, one is not quite convinced by the apparent harmonic anomalies; the intent of passages like the refrain of [72] [Autre Rondeau] (assuming it is notated correctly in its two sources) is indeed puzzling. Yet in spite of this and other stylistic weaknesses—the startling chromaticism in upper voices and the questionable voice-leading in lower parts when modulating—there is considerable competence in Draghi's handling of genres and much skilful variety in his treatment of texture, counterpoint, rhythm, and melody. His keyboard style compares favorably with that of his English contemporaries, exploiting a wide compass and thick sonorities in ways that demonstrate his awareness of the harpsichord's potential and of the natural physical gestures of the harpsichordist. The pieces also exhibit a remarkably wide emotional range, from the seriousness and intensity of those in B minor, to the gaiety and spontaneity of some of the jauntier aires. The music in this volume represents an estimable level of achievement for a "lesser" composer and should provide rewarding exploration for the musician of today.

Sources

This edition of Draghi's harpsichord music has been assembled from a single print and several manuscripts. The print, one of the few in England at the time to be devoted to one composer, probably represents what Draghi wished to preserve as a testimony of his life's work. But the manuscripts are of considerable importance to the study of his harpsichord music, not only because they contain more than half his output for the instrument, but also because a large number of pieces in them are of no less musical worth than the finest ones in the print.

The sources consulted for transcription and the sigla by which they are identified in the following discussion, are given below.[16] (The bracketed numerals are those assigned for the present edition.)

Ed. 1707	*Six Select Sutes* [sic] *of Lessons for the Harpsicord in Six Severall Keys, Consisting of Preludes, Allemands, Corrants, Sarabands, Arietts, Minuets, & Jiggs, Compos'd by Signr Giovani Baptista Draghi* (London: Walsh, n.d.). First advertised in the *Post Man*, 4–6 February 1707. [1]–[37]
	Copies (RISM A/1, D 3491)
	London, British Library (title page in manuscript)
	Oxford, Christ Church Library
	Cambridge, Rowe Music Library, King's College
	Durham, Cathedral Library
	Brussels, Conservatoire royal de musique, Bibliothèque
	Boston, Public Library
	New Haven, Yale University, Library of the School of Music
	Cambridge, Fitzwilliam Museum (later edition?)
Lbl 1	London, British Library, MS Egerton 2959. Keyboard manuscript, ca. 1700. Formerly belonged to John Gostling and W. H. Cummings. [26]
Lbl 2	London, British Library, MS Add. 22099. Keyboard manuscript, 1704–7. [85]
Lbl 3	London, British Library, MS Add. 39569. "Recueil de pièces choisies pour le Clauessin, 1702, William Babel." [1], [65]–[73]
Lbl 4	London, British Library, MS Add. 41205. Keyboard manuscript, first half of the eighteenth century. Owned by W. A. Barrett, said to be in the hand of John Barrett (doubtful). [70]
Lbl 5	London, British Library, MS Add. 52363. Keyboard manuscript, "Elizabeth Batt [Barrett?] 1704." [4], [74]–[78]
Ob	Oxford, Bodleian Library, Music School MS E. 397. Keyboard and song manuscript, early eighteenth century. Note on flyleaf: "Miss Millane begune August ye 10 1747," but date of compilation probably earlier. [45], [46], [49]
Och 1	Oxford, Christ Church Library, MS 1003. Keyboard manuscript, ca. 1630–ca. 1685. Owned by Richard Goodson, Sr. [62], [63]
Och 2	Oxford, Christ Church Library, MS 1177. Keyboard manuscript, ca. 1660–ca. 1690. Owned by Richard Goodson, Sr. [26], [62]–[64]
Cfm 1	Cambridge, Fitzwilliam Museum, Music MS 652 (52.B.6). Score, 1702 and later. For-

merly owned by W. H. Cummings. (Partial Draghi autograph?) [52], [55], [57], [59]–[61]

Cfm 2   Cambridge, Fitzwilliam Museum, Music MS 653 (52.B.7). Keyboard manuscript, first half of the eighteenth century. Formerly owned by W. H. Cummings. [70], [71]

T   Tenbury Wells, St. Michael's College, MS 1508. Keyboard manuscript. "Ce livre Arpartient a gm. Babel 1701 London" (now in the Bodleian Library, Oxford). [1], [69]

CDp   Cardiff, Public Library, Mackworth Collection MS 1.39(j). Bass part and keyboard manuscript (reverse end), early eighteenth century. [79]–[81]

En   Edinburgh, National Library of Scotland, Inglis 94 MS 3343. Keyboard manuscript, ca. 1695. [82]–[84]

Bc   Brussels, Conservatoire royal de musique, Bibliothèque, MS XY.15 139.Z. Keyboard manuscript, 1687. [26]

Wc   Washington, Library of Congress, MS M21 M185. Keyboard manuscript of toccatas, sonatas, and suites, ca. 1705. [1]–[6], [27], [38]–[53], [64]

U   Urbana, Library of the University of Illinois at Urbana-Champaign, MS x786.4108/M319. Keyboard manuscript, 1701. [54]–[58]

LAuc   Los Angeles, William Andrews Clark Memorial Library, University of California at Los Angeles, D173 M4 H295 1690 bound. Keyboard manuscript, ca. 1695. [65]–[68], [72], [73]

The edition of 1707 presents thirty-seven pieces arranged in six suites; one suite has seven movements, the rest six. The number of movements in each suite is exceptionally large when compared with the three or four movements usual in the printed collections of Blow, Purcell, and Clarke. The engraving is neat and clear, though not entirely free of mistakes. In the New Haven copy of Ed. 1707, notes and rests have been added in one or two places by a contemporary hand, and it is tempting to speculate that these might be the composer's own emendations. This was the copy used for transcription, and all of the handwritten additions are accounted for in the Critical Notes.

The Washington manuscript (Wc) contains twenty-four pieces attributed to Draghi, the largest number in any of the manuscript sources. It is a collection of toccatas and sonatas by Italian composers, together with suites and miscellaneous pieces mostly by Draghi and Francis Forcer (ca. 1650–ca. 1704). There is also a transcription of Purcell's overture to *Timon of Athens*, Z. T691, and a previously unknown "Cybelle," possibly also by Forcer. All of the E-minor pieces and one D-minor piece in Ed. 1707 are also found in Wc, and the close similarity of the readings suggests a relationship between the two sources. For example, the Lbl 5 version of [4] The Complaint shows a number of melodic and harmonic variants when compared to the reading of Ed. 1707; no such variants exist in the Wc version. A few more ornaments are to be found in Wc than in Ed. 1707, and some of the mistakes engraved in the print read correctly in the manuscript. However, such features as unconventional stemming and beaming are often identical in both sources. One might infer that the seven pieces in Wc concordant with Ed. 1707 were copied from the print, with ornaments added and mistakes corrected. It is equally possible, however, that the manuscript provided one source of pieces for the print, especially in view of the presence in Wc of many other pieces by Draghi not printed, including one extra E-minor piece ([40] Ayre). These pieces may have been rejected for the edition because of length (e.g., [39] Trumpet) or unusual key (the C-minor group), or because a sufficient number of pieces in a particular key (e.g., D minor) were available from another source. I am therefore inclined to suppose that the manuscript precedes the print—hence, my proposal of ca. 1705 as the date for Wc.

The Urbana manuscript (U), though only about half the size of Wc, contains a similar repertory. It also includes several toccatas by Italian composers, three of which are concordant with Wc. The group of five pieces in G minor by Draghi found in U provides us with some glimpses of a composer "borrowing from himself," i.e., using identical material in different pieces. Compare, for example, the G-minor Courante in U ([56a]) with that in Ed. 1707 ([15]): they are nearly identical for the first three measures but differ thereafter. Similarly, [1] Prelude and [54] Prelude (though in different keys) open with the same figure and have similar second measures, but are otherwise different pieces. Since U dates from 1701, it may also have been a source from which Draghi drew in compiling pieces for Ed. 1707, this time revising material and transposing as he saw fit.

Particular interest attaches to Cfm 1 because the six Draghi pieces that begin the manuscript may be either in the composer's hand or in the hand of a person closely associated with him. The pieces carry only the ascription "B," but the first piece ([52] [Saraband]) is concordant with Wc. This suggests that "B" stands for "Baptist," and such a cryptic signature would not be uncommon for a composer referring to himself. Furthermore, the hand of both music and text is identical with that of the manuscript in the Royal College of Music containing Draghi's St. Cecilia's Day Ode of 1687, and this manuscript has all the earmarks of a composer's or conductor's score—actual singers' names designated for particular passages, directions for performance, instrumentation, etc.[17] While a mere initial stands for the composer's name in Cfm 1, remarkably complete information is given about the time of copying: "Thursday, Feb. ye 13th: 1701/2 allmost 2 a Clock." Interestingly, these six pieces are not arranged as a suite or suites (four different keys are represented), and the last piece contains the Italianate designation *tr* instead of the English shake sign. The manuscript also contains the same almand and "Arietta" as U, with similar readings. Thus, it is evident that Ed. 1707, Wc, U, and the first part of Cfm 1, compiled within six or seven years of each other, are related sources all of which might possibly have originated within the orbit of Draghi himself.

The Christ Church manuscripts (Och 1 and Och 2) are probably the earliest sources of Draghi's harpsichord music, and the same D-minor suite ([62]–[64]) is found at the beginning of the reverse end of both. (Och 1 has only the Almaine and a few measures of the Corant.) A further Allmand ([26]), unattributed in Och 2, eventually found its way into Ed. 1707.

The Babell manuscripts (Lbl 3 and T), considered together with LAuc, present an interesting connection to Draghi's harpsichord music. The first two are large collections of pieces by both English and Continental composers, in the hand of Charles Babell, father of William (whose name is stamped on the covers of both manuscripts). The elder Babell had already made several volumes of partbooks of trios between 1697 and 1700. In Lbl 3 are ten pieces by Draghi, nine of them comprising a "5me Suite en B mineur/Pieces de Mr. Baptiste." The Gigue from this suite is also in T, and six of the other eight pieces are also found anonymously in LAuc. This last is a small volume dating from several years earlier than the Babell manuscripts. A cursory glance at its contents immediately suggests a connection between it and Lbl 3; both manuscripts contain Purcell's Suites in G major (Z. 660) and F major (Z. 669), and both omit the F-major Prelude. Closer scrutiny reveals internal evidence that LAuc was one of the sources used by Babell in compiling Lbl 3. Several duplications of misplaced accidentals and of faulty spacing occur, and voices seem to have been inadvertently omitted here and there. (See Critical Notes for [66] [Allemande], m. 34, and [67] [Courante], m. 4.) The B-minor pieces contained in LAuc, Lbl 3, and T are among the finest of Draghi's harpsichord works, exhibiting as they do a highly developed *style brisé* seldom encountered in the English harpsichord repertory.

The other principal sources are Lbl 5, CDp, En, and Lbl 2, accounting in all for twelve additional pieces. Concordances only are contained in Lbl 1, Lbl 4, Ob, Och 1, Cfm 2, T, and Bc, although [45] Prelud[e] from Ob and [70] Allemande from Cfm 2 are included in this edition for the sake of comparison with their principal sources.

Authenticity

The ascriptions most frequently given for Draghi's pieces in manuscript are "Signor Baptist," "Mr. Baptist," and merely "Baptist" (or variations thereof). Hawkins warned that "Signor Baptist means uniformly Baptist Draghi, and not Baptist Lully, as some have supposed,"[18] but since this is not strictly true, he himself confused Draghi and Lully on occasion.[19] In fact, the various "Baptist" ascriptions found in English sources can refer to either Draghi, Lully, or indeed such other composers as Jean-Baptiste Loeillet (1680–1730), who settled in London about 1705. The only sure way of determining authenticity of pieces in these cases is through accurately ascribed concordances. Failing that, attributions must be made on the basis of other considerations. Lully is not known to have written any original harpsichord music,

and most of what exists for the instrument has been traced to his dramatic works. None of Draghi's harpsichord pieces, on the other hand, have been found in versions for any other medium. In En one finds pieces by both Lully and Draghi, but the scribe carefully differentiated between the two by identifying the former as "French Baptist" or "Baptist Lully of France," and the latter as "Senior Baptist." The Lully pieces are arrangements from *Thésée* and *Le Triomphe de l'Amour*.

Particular stylistic formulas frequently employed by Draghi have helped in attributing some unascribed pieces. One such formula is an immediately recognizable melodic figure found in the uppermost voice after a cadence is reached at the end of a section. The figure is characterized by a rise from the tonic to the supertonic, then down to the dominant, and back up to the tonic (sometimes the supertonic is omitted). Three unascribed pieces—[62] Almaine, [63] Corant, and [81] [Almand]—were identified in this way. (Cf. similar cadential figures in [8] Allmand, [9] Corrant, [14] Allmand, [26] Allmand, [42] Allemande, [53] Almond, and many others.) Note that the Cfm 2 version of [70] Allemande has the figure in the last measure of the piece, whereas the Lbl 3 version does not. This last instance confirmed the "Mr. Baptiste" ascription for all the B-minor pieces in Lbl 3 as a reference to Draghi.

The present edition does not include the famous C-minor ground from Henry Playford's *Second Part of Musick's Hand-maid* (1689), long thought by some to be a work of Draghi.[20] This attribution seems to have originated with Thurston Dart, who identified a three-part version of the ground in British Library, MS Add. 22100, beginning with the text "Scocca pur tutti tuoi strali" and ascribed to "Mr. Baptist."[21] In spite of the fact that this is expanded to "Sr Baptist Lully" in the table of contents, Dart, probably influenced by the Italian words and the abbreviation "Sr," felt compelled to attribute it to Draghi. He was, apparently, unaware of the various arrangements of "Scocca pur" in French sources, including some of those compiled by Lully's own copyist, André Danican Philidor. Documentary evidence further suggests that the original "Scocca pur" is, after all, associated with Lully and not with Draghi.[22] Like other melodies imported from France (e.g., the Cibell tune), the melody of "Scocca pur" became extremely popular in England. D'Urfey wrote English words to it and included them, without printing the music, in *Songs Compleat, Pleasant and Divertive* (1719). The subtitle, "English Words made to a Famous Italian Ayre, call'd Scoca puero," indicates that the popularity of the tune made inclusion of the music unnecessary. Regarding the keyboard version, we know that Purcell was closely associated with the production of *Musick's Hand-maid II*, as stated in the preface: "the Impression being carefully Revised and Corrected by the said Mr. Henry Purcell." The ground also appears in Och 2, grouped together with several pieces by Purcell, including his C-minor Ground, Z. T681. Zimmerman pointed out that the ground bass of the piece is exactly the same as that of the great Sonata VI of Four Parts, published posthumously in 1697.[23] And the keyboard style of the ground is similar to that of grounds transcribed for keyboard by Purcell, including "A New Ground" in E minor (Z. T682), also in *Musick's Hand-maid II*. Does this constitute evidence that Purcell was attracted by the ground and may himself have arranged the keyboard version? Given that no logical connection to it can be traced to Draghi, the authorship of this piece remains a subject for further enquiry.

Two pieces by Draghi in Ed. 1707 are differently ascribed in other sources, these being [1] Prelude (to King in T) and [26] Allmand (to Blow in Lbl 1 and Bc).

Editorial Methods

Choice and treatment of sources

Each piece in this volume was transcribed from a single source. For pieces transmitted in more than one source, a principal source was chosen on the basis of the composer's authority (e.g., the print, autograph) and/or preferability of the text. The remaining sources for each piece are designated as either a "secondary source" or "other source(s)." A secondary source is one in which a definite relationship with the principal source, implied in the first instance by similar readings, has been determined. These relationships are summarized in table 1. All secondary source information which *adds* to that in the principal source, such as additional notes, rests, accidentals and ornaments, is given in square brackets. A comment in the Critical Notes will differentiate between secondary source readings and editorial additions. All secondary source information which *emends* that in the principal source, such as differing notes, note values,

and other small variants, is accounted for in the Critical Notes. It is thus possible to reconstruct the texts of both the principal and secondary sources using the Critical Notes, although the text itself reflects the principal source only. For all other sources, only a statement in the Critical Notes as to how their readings generally differ from the principal source is given. In two cases different readings of entire pieces have been included to afford instructive comparisons: [45] Prelud[e], which presents sixteenth-note rather than eighth-note subdivisions of the beat, and [70] Allemande, showing enriched textures in a later source.

Pieces are ordered more or less by principal source, beginning with the print, then on through the manuscripts approximately in order of importance to Draghi's works. Ordering within sources is preserved with one or two exceptions (see Critical Notes). Note that the same pieces often appear with interchangeable companion pieces from one source to another, and that pieces grouped together in a source do not always make up a suite (e.g., Cfm 1). The numbering of the pieces is editorial.

Titles

Titles are given as in the principal sources. While antiquated typography (e.g., *I* for *J*) has been silently modernized, and abbreviated forms (e.g., *Ital:*) have been expanded, no attempt has been made to regularize spelling. (All source inscriptions are reported exactly in the Critical Notes.) Titles appearing in square brackets have been supplied either on the authority of the secondary source or editorially, in which case orthography follows the general usage reflected by the principal source.

TABLE 1
Principal and Secondary Sources

Principal Source	Secondary Source	Relationship	Rationale for Choice	Transcription
Ed. 1707	Wc	Part of Wc was possibly chosen for inclusion in Ed. 1707	Print probably has composer authority	[1]–[6], [27]
Cfm 1	Wc	Both probably originated within the composer's circle	Possible composer autograph	[52]
Cfm 1	U	Both probably originated within the composer's circle	Possible composer autograph	[55], [57]
Och 2	Och 1	The same two pieces are found beginning the reverse end of both volumes	Clearer, more professional hand	[65], [66]
LAuc	Lbl 3	Part of LAuc was copied into Lbl 3	More complete text, using more definitive English ornamental signs	[68]–[71], [75] [76]
Lbl 3	T	Both are in the hand of Charles Babell	More complete text	[72]

Clefs, key signatures, time signatures

Clefs and disposition of notes on staves are modernized to conform with standard keyboard score. All key signatures and time signatures are original.

Repetition

It is assumed that both sections of binary-form pieces are always repeated, and the universality of this assumption may in itself explain why no uniform manner of indicating repetition exists in early keyboard sources. Purcell's "Rules for Graces" state that the double bar "set down at ye end of every Strain . . . imports you must play ye Strain twice." In the sources these double bars do divide binary-form pieces, but they are also used to mark ends of sections in non-binary forms where repetition is not logical (e.g., [84] A Ground, m. 16). I have therefore employed the modern repeat sign (double bar and dots) only for binary-form pieces, the first strain of rondo-form pieces, and any other place where repetition is indicated in the source by a melodic pattern leading to the beginning of a section or piece.

Two other kinds of repetition occur; one is the "petite reprise" (i.e., repetition of the last few measures of a piece), the other is the repetition of an entire piece (again indicated in the sources by a melodic pattern leading to the beginning). I have adopted two sizes of the sign 𝄋, the smaller size designating "petite reprise." (Note that [57] [Arietta] requires both types of repetition.) The sign is placed at the beginning of the first, and at the end of the last measure to be repeated, much as it is done in the original sources.

Occasionally, the source does not make it clear to us how to end a piece, giving only a melodic pattern to lead back to a repeat, but not one with which to close. Usually a logical ending pattern can be found somewhere in either the first- or second-ending measures. Consequently, rather than provide an editorial ending, I have placed the sign [fine] in the general vicinity of such a pattern. The player may wish to use this ending, but it is easy to imagine an eighteenth-century player inventing one of his own, consistent with the style of the piece. There is no reason why the modern player should not also feel free to do so.

Notational conventions

While the stemming of notes has been tacitly conventionalized, flagging and beaming as in the principal source have been followed literally in spite of many apparent irregularities. This policy arises from the difficulty of distinguishing between beaming that implies articulation, and mere idiosyncracies of the engraver/scribe. Presentation of original beaming also reflects more of the nature of the principal source, and in most cases it should not detract from facility in reading. I would suggest that all implications of original beaming in keyboard sources have not been fully explored by performers, theorists, and historians, and the study may one day prove a vital one.

The rhythmic figure 𝅘𝅥𝅭 𝅘𝅥𝅰𝅘𝅥𝅰𝅘𝅥 (or 𝅘𝅥𝅮 𝅘𝅥𝅰𝅘𝅥𝅰𝅘𝅥 or 𝄾 𝅘𝅥𝅰𝅘𝅥𝅰𝅘𝅥) is a familiar one to performers of baroque music and is frequently found in Draghi sources. It reflects the variable duration of the rhythmic dot of Draghi's time, opposing the modern rule of theory that the value of the dot is always half that of the note preceding it. To render the figure in modern terms (e.g., 𝅘𝅥𝅭 𝅘𝅥𝅰𝅘𝅥𝅰𝅘𝅥) would belie an important rhythmic implication of the original—that which clearly conveys the upbeat character of the thirty-second-notes, and the absence of the slightest accent on the initial one. The original notation of dotted rhythms has therefore been preserved throughout.

Ties added from secondary sources or editorially, are dashed; the former are identified in the Critical Notes.

Errors

In passages that are questionable on musical grounds, it is not always easy to distinguish between what were quite possibly the composer's intentions and what were errors of the scribe or engraver. Readings judged to have resulted from the latter have been corrected in this edition and accounted for in the Critical Notes. Otherwise, I have made no attempt at editorial reconstruction, although some suggestions are offered in the pertinent critical notes. In such cases the player is invited to exercise his own critical judgment and to reach his own decisions.

Accidentals

The use of accidental marks follows modern convention. Those in brackets are either added by authority of the secondary source (indicated in the Critical Notes) or editorially. Occasionally an accidental is found uniquely in a source other than the principal or secondary one. When such an accidental corrects an error or results in a reading preferable to that of the principal source, it is incorporated as editorial. Cautionary accidentals are editorial and are enclosed in parentheses.

Ornaments

The sources of Draghi's harpsichord music are not all in agreement as to the type of ornamental signs employed. For example, Lbl 3 and T use signs found more frequently in French than in English harpsichord music. However, Ed. 1707 contains signs derived from the most important of the surviving English tables of ornaments of the period—Purcell's "Rules for Graces" (in *A Choice Collection of Lessons*, 1696, and elsewhere). The one exception is the "beat," in which the French *pincé* ✲ is substituted for ∾ . For the sake of consistency, the Ed. 1707 ornaments are employed throughout this edition except in the case of [61] Almand from Cfm 1. Here, unexpectedly, the sign *tr* replaces ⫽, and because the source may be a composer autograph, this sign has been retained in the transcription.

The French *tremblement* sign (∿), employed by Charles Babell in Lbl 3 and T, presents a problem for adaptation to an English sign, because it does not differentiate between a shake and a "plain note and shake" (i.e., ⫽ and ⫽). Fortunately, in two of the three pieces for which Lbl 3 is the principal source, the *tremblement* sign could be checked against concordances in Cfm 2 and Lbl

4, where English signs are employed, and these have been collated without comment. In the case of [69] Gigue, present in Lbl 3 and T only, all *tremblements* become shakes without the "plain note."

In Cfm 1 and U, both forefalls (╱) and backfalls (╲) are indicated by the latter sign. Thus, forefall signs are given tacitly where logic dictates, as in most ascending lines.

All bracketed ornaments are added by authority of the secondary source. It was decided that no editorial ornaments should be given, since these might intrude upon the province of the performer. Inflected "beat" signs—i.e., those with small accidentals over or under the signs to indicate inflection of the auxiliary note—are peculiar to some sources. These are retained and, if they are found in a secondary source only, are enclosed in square brackets. In transcriptions from sources that normally employ "beat" inflections, editorial ones are added where they seem to be missing; these are also bracketed, and they are accounted for in the Critical Notes.

Notes on Performance

What follows are a few comments specifically related to some aspects of the performance of Draghi's harpsichord music. These comments may be amplified by the excellent detailed discussion of all matters concerning tempo, rhythm, and style generally appropriate to keyboard performance of this period, found in the Introduction to Howard Ferguson's *Early English Keyboard Music*. I also include a brief account of keyboard instruments in England at this time, as well as some thoughts on the choice of instrument for performing this music.

Interpretation of ornaments and other signs

In English sources no features of notation are so inconsistently handled as the number and placement of ornamental signs. A glance through this volume will reveal that ornaments abound in some sources (e.g., Wc), while in others they are practically non-existent (e.g., CDp). It is rare to find two sources of the same piece, even copied by the same scribe, in which all ornaments coincide exactly. While it is instructive to observe where and when ornaments occur in the sources, the player should in no way feel bound by the ornamental signs given here and is encouraged to add his own ornamentation as freely as good taste will permit.

The "Rules for Graces" were sought out for guidance in the interpretation of all ornamental signs. Only one sign, the long diagonal line rising from left to right (e.g., [5] Aire, m. 7), is not treated there. This probably signifies a slide of three notes akin to the long slur in French music (cf. d'Anglebert's "Marques des agréments" in his *Pièces de clavecin*, 1689) and to the German *Schleifer*. Table 2, proposed on the basis of Purcell's "Rules for Graces," should clarify the interpretation of all signs found in these transcriptions.

Two signs other than ornamental ones are also found. One is the slur over or under two or more notes, which is

Ornament	Name	Interpretation
Ed. 1707		"Rules for Graces"
	Shake	
	Beat	[really]
	Plain note and shake	
	Forefall	
	Backfall	
	Shake turned	
	Slur	
	Slide*	
Cfm 1		
([61] Almand)		
tr		

TABLE 2
Interpretation of Ornaments

*Not explained in "Rules for Graces."

rare. From French usage (e.g., Rameau) one may gather that this instructs the player to hold all slurred notes for the slur's duration. The other sign is ⸶·, found in Wc (see [39] Trumpet, *passim*, and [42] Allemande, mm. 20 and 23). Its meaning here is obscure, but it could refer to the keyboard manual playing the "single" set of strings. This is hinted at in mm. 33 and 35 of [39] Trumpet with the words "Up[pe]r Sett" and "Lower Sett." Registration indications of this sort are actually more typical of English organ than of English harpsichord music. For example, a Voluntary by Christopher Gibbons in British Library MS Add. 31446, fol. 24v, contains a "Trumpet" section with the indications "Trumpet" (i.e., trumpet stop) and "sing[le]," the latter similarly placed as in Draghi's Trumpet. This is not to suggest that the piece *must* be played on the organ, as the keyboard style itself is as suited here to the harpsichord as it is in Draghi's other harpsichord pieces.

Notational style and rhythm

A number of interesting notational peculiarities evident in the sources give rise to some observations concerning rhythmic inequality in English keyboard music. The French practice of playing pairs of notes of equal duration unequally is by now well known. English keyboard sources from the time of Locke's *Melothesia* (1673) to the first quarter of the eighteenth century reveal numerous passages, and sometimes whole pieces, notated in dotted rhythms, almost certainly directing players to imitate French *notes inégales*. Where a mixture of equally and unequally notated pairs occurs within a piece, the question is raised as to what extent this represents intentional variety as opposed to mere notational inconsistency. For example, [2] Allmand contains passages in equal sixteenths, equal sixteenths slurred in pairs, dotted sixteenths followed by thirty-seconds, and thirty-seconds followed by dotted sixteenths. These four separate notational patterns may not be the result of scribal or editorial indifference, especially since in many cases the kind of notation employed can be explained by the nature of the passage itself (e.g., slurred pairs in conjunct descending motion, mm. 26–28; thirty-seconds followed by dotted sixteenths in descending thirds, mm. 31, 32; etc.). One cannot necessarily assume, in these patterns, that rhythms should be altered at all in performance. Elsewhere, as in quicker pieces where the variety of notated rhythms is less extreme (e.g., all eighth-notes with occasional dotted eighths and sixteenths), the player may be receiving another kind of direction: the dotted figures may be an invitation to play all of the equal eighths unequally as well. Indeed, the subtle differences between equal rhythms and variously rendered rhythms, perceptible in the Allmand, would not be effectively heard in pieces at a faster tempo. Therefore, in slower movements where a variety of rhythmic notation occurs, the player should first determine what, if any, relationships exist between certain notational patterns and patterns of melodic motion. He may then wish to project such relationships by adhering to values as notated. Otherwise, and particularly in many of the quicker movements, he should not be afraid to play entire pieces in unequal rhythm, just as a culturally enlightened Englishman of Draghi's time, with his fondness of French habit, might have done. Finally, pieces that in French music would favor *notes égales*—e.g., very fast movements or those containing certain passages of disjunct motion—would favor equality of rhythm here as well.

Instrument

Relatively few native English harpsichords from the sixteenth and seventeenth centuries have survived to the present day, and the lack of documentary evidence suggesting lively activity in English instrument building at the time leads one to suspect that at first a tradition of importing instruments existed. By the middle of the seventeenth century, however, some English makers were flourishing.

The most famous English builders around Draghi's time were Charles Haward (fl. 1660–87), John Player (ca. 1634–ca. 1705), and the Thomas Hitchcocks (one fl. 1660–1700, the other lived ca. 1685–ca. 1735).[24] Almost all of their known instruments were of the spinet or virginal variety, and Queen Anne is said to have owned and prized a virginal by Haward.[25] These small instruments had only one manual and one set of strings. Those surviving today show many Italian characteristics, in particular the short scaling (i.e., sounding length of strings), which yields a dry, evanescent sound, brilliant in attack and rich in partials. Their ranges vary, but the most common is GG-c''' with either a short or broken bass octave. While some contemporary sources hint at the presence of larger instruments,[26] most evidence indicates that the norm for seventeenth-century England was the small spinet or virginal with only one set of strings.

If Draghi intended his music to be played outside the most elite circle of instrument owners, he would have to write music capable of being played on these fairly simple instruments. Apart from the two pieces where manual changes may be indicated, all of Draghi's harpsichord works are accessible on one manual. None require a note lower than GG or higher than c''', and all can be played on instruments with the short, broken, or chromatic octave in the bass. (See also the Critical Note to [5] Aire, m. 7.) The drier-sounding instrument lends itself particularly well to the brilliant passage work in some of the preludes, in the jigs, and in the second section of [38] Toccata, and adds sparkle to corants and the quicker aires. One can also imagine beautiful results with the slower movements in the hands of a sensitive player capable of exploiting the expressive *style brisé* to its fullest effect.

However, it would be wide of the mark to insist that these small single-register instruments are the only ones suitable for the performance of Draghi's music. The expressive possibilities offered by a more elaborate instrument, especially the various tone colors of single and combined registers, would certainly be an asset in contrasting one movement with another. In short, when playing English harpsichord music of this period, we are not faced—to the extent we might be in, say, French music—with the necessity of choosing a single most appropriate instrument. The uniquely idiomatic keyboard writing of French composers often leads one to believe that they had a particular type of instrument in mind, and such an instrument is to be preferred over all others for their music. But in the performance of Draghi's harpsichord music, satisfactory results can be achieved on any good plucked-string keyboard instrument, including the smallest and simplest.

Critical Notes

For each piece, sources are indicated by sigla (see Sources), followed by page or folio number and inscriptions, if any. When necessary, inscriptions found at the head of a piece are separated by a slash from those found at its end. All discrepancies between the principal source and the present edition or between principal and secondary sources, as well as further readings in other sources, are reported here as outlined under Editorial Methods. The following abbreviations are used to identify voices:

    s = upper staff, upward stem
    a = upper staff, downward stem
    t = lower staff, upward stem
    b = lower staff, downward stem

Where only a single voice is present in a staff, it is designated *r.h.* for upper staff or *l.h.* for lower staff. Pitches are identified according to the system c' = middle C.

[1] Prelude

PRINCIPAL SOURCE: Ed. 1707, p. 1, "Prelude"

SECONDARY SOURCE: Wc, pp. 56–57, "Sute of Lesson Dell Sign^re Baptist Draghi" "Prelude"

OTHER SOURCES: (1) Lbl 3, p. 32, "2me Prelude"; (2) T, fol. 21v, "en E. 5me Suitte" "Prelude Mr. King"

(Cf. [54] Prelude)

Lbl 3 and T have an additional measure at the end, further defining the E-minor chord.

M. 4, t, note 1, quarter-note in both sources. M. 8, s, note 5, ornament in Ed. 1707 only. M. 9, l.h., dotted half-note in Ed. 1707 and half tied to quarter-note in Wc. The incomplete final measure could be an indication to proceed to the Allmand without pause.

[2] Allmand

PRINCIPAL SOURCE: Ed. 1707, pp. 2–3, "Allmand"

SECONDARY SOURCE: Wc, pp. 58–61, "Allemande"

M. 3, r.h., note 9, ornament in Ed. 1707 only; t, note 1, e′ in Wc. M. 4, s, note 1, ornament in Ed. 1707 only; l.h., beat 2, dotted eighth followed by sixteenth in Wc. M. 8, a, beat 4, in Wc no initial rest, e′ is eighth-note. M. 9, s, note 10, eighth-note in Wc. M. 12, r.h., note 1, tie in Ed. 1707 only, note 4, sixteenth-note in Wc, note 7, eighth-note in both sources; a, beat 4, g′ is sixteenth-note in Wc. M. 13, s, note 1, tie in Ed. 1707 only, note 4, eighth-note in Ed. 1707; a, note 3, eighth-note in both sources. M. 14, t, notes 2 and 3, lower notes in Wc, note 4, lower note, g in Ed. 1707; b, note 3, eighth-note in Wc. M. 15, s, note 1, ornament in Ed. 1707 only; a, beat 4 in Ed. 1707 only. M. 16, b, beat 4, first note, g-sharp in Ed. 1707. M. 18, r.h., note 1, ornament in Ed. 1707 only; in Wc, r.h., note 7 is quarter-note, note 10, sixteenth-note, beat 4, last two notes are dotted eighth followed by sixteenth-note. M. 20, r.h., note 4, ornament inflection editorial, note 6, "plain note" sign in Ed. 1707 only. M. 24, a, note 2 in Ed. 1707 only. M. 25, t, note 2, a in Ed. 1707. M. 26, r.h., beat 3, sixteenth-notes in Wc. M. 27, s, beat 3, lower note, e′ in Ed. 1707; l.h., notes 9 and 10, sixteenth-notes in Wc. M. 28, b, note 1, quarter-note in both sources. M. 29, s, note 3, sharp in Wc. M. 30, a, note 1, tie in Wc, note 2, e′-sharp in Wc, note 3, d′-natural in Wc. M. 31, s, note 1, ornament in Ed. 1707 only (inflection editorial), note 3, ornament in Ed. 1707 only, notes 5–12, alternating dotted sixteenths and thirty-seconds in Wc; a, beats 2 and 3 in Wc; t, note 1, eighth-note in Wc. M. 32, a, beat 3, tie in Ed. 1707 only.

[3] Corrant

PRINCIPAL SOURCE: Ed. 1707, p. 4, "Corrant"

SECONDARY SOURCE: Wc, pp. 62–63, "Courante"

M. 1, r.h., note 3, ornament in Ed. 1707 only. M. 3, r.h., note 2, ornament in Ed. 1707 only. M. 7, r.h., note 9, ornament in Ed. 1707 only. Mm. 8 and 9, s, note 1, ornament in Ed. 1707 only. M. 11, r.h., note 5, "plain note" sign in Ed. 1707 only. M. 12, r.h., note 3, ornament in Ed. 1707 only, note 8, "plain note" sign in Ed. 1707 only. M. 15, r.h., note 4, ornament in Ed. 1707 only (inflection editorial); b, notes 1 and 2, half-notes in both sources. M. 17, r.h., note 1, ornament in Ed. 1707 only. M. 18, r.h., note 6, "plain note" sign in Ed. 1707 only.

[4] The Complaint

PRINCIPAL SOURCE: Ed. 1707, p. 5, "The Complaint"

SECONDARY SOURCE: Wc, pp. 64–65, "Sarabande The Complaint"

OTHER SOURCE: Lbl 5, pp. 96–97, "complaint"/"baptist" "slow"

Lbl 5 presents a few melodic variants, and suppresses the dissonance in m. 11.

M. 5, t, beat 1, rest in Wc. M. 6, a, note 1 in Ed. 1707 only. M. 15, r.h., note 1, tie in Ed. 1707 only; slur over first three notes in Wc. M. 24, r.h., slurs in Wc. M. 26, s, note 1, tie in Wc. M. 27, b, half-note in both sources. M. 32, s, beat 3, "plain note" sign in Ed. 1707 only.

[5] Aire

PRINCIPAL SOURCE: Ed. 1707, p. 6, "Aire"

SECONDARY SOURCE: Wc, pp. 66–67, "Bouree"

M. 4, r.h., note 1, ornament in Ed. 1707 only. M. 7, t, beat 4, f-sharp instead of rest in Wc. This implies an instrument with the C/E short octave, although other pieces in Wc have notes lower than C. M. 15, r.h., note 1, ornament in Ed. 1707 only (inflection editorial). M. 19, b, beat 2, dotted eighth followed by sixteenth in Wc. M. 20, r.h., note 6, "plain note" sign in Ed. 1707 only. M. 22, l.h., notes 5 and 6, quarter-notes in Ed. 1707.

[6] Jigg

PRINCIPAL SOURCE: Ed. 1707, p. 7, "Iigg"

SECONDARY SOURCE: Wc, pp. 68–70, "Gigue"

M. 5, t, beat 4, quarter-note in Ed. 1707; b, eighth-note on beat 6 in Ed. 1707. M. 9, b, quarter-notes in both sources. M. 11, t, note 2, g′ in both sources. M. 17, a, note 1, quarter-note in Ed. 1707. M. 19, b, beat 4, quarter-note in both sources. M. 21, r.h., note 4, ornament inflection is editorial. M. 23, r.h., note 3, ornament in Ed. 1707 only. M. 25, s, note 4, ornament in Ed. 1707 only. M. 27, b, beat 4, quarter-note in Ed. 1707. M. 37, r.h., note 5, ornament in Ed. 1707 only. M. 39, b, note 4, quarter-note in Ed. 1707. M. 41, l.h., note 1, dotted quarter-notes in Ed. 1707. M. 43, r.h., note 4, ornament inflection is editorial; l.h., quarter-note followed by rests in Wc.

[7] Prelude

SOURCE: Ed. 1707, p. 8, "Prelude"

[8] Allmand

SOURCE: Ed. 1707, pp. 9–10, "Allmand"

M. 6, r.h., note 9, c"-natural. M. 11, t, final note, eighth-note; b, beat 4, quarter-note. M. 16, r.h., beat 2, c" and d" are sixteenth-notes. M. 17, r.h., beat 2, dotted quarter-note. M. 22, r.h., beat 2, lowest note is e'. M. 27, t, final note, eighth-note; b, beat 4, quarter-note.

[9] Corrant

SOURCE: Ed. 1707, p. 11, "Corrant"

M. 3, r.h., third half-note beat, lower note is undotted quarter-note. M. 5, a, note 1, half-note. M. 6, b, note 2, quarter-note. Mm. 7, 8, and 17, l.h., final quarter beat, quarter-note.

[10] Saraband

SOURCE: Ed. 1707, p.12, "Saraband"

M. 8, b, half-note. M. 15, b, beat 3, d. M. 24, s, half-note.

[11] Aire

SOURCE: Ed. 1707, p. 12, "Aire"

[12] The Hunting Tune

SOURCE: Ed. 1707, p. 13, "The Hunting Tune"

M. 12, l.h., note 1, quarter-note. M. 14, r.h., note 12, thirty-second-note.

[13] Prelude

SOURCE: Ed. 1707, p. 14, "Prelude"

M. 8, r.h., note 13, e"-flat. M. 13, a, note 2, a'.

[14] Allmand

SOURCE: Ed. 1707, p. 15, "Allmand"

M. 8, t, beats 3 and 4, quarter- and eighth-rests vertically aligned followed by dotted eighth g and sixteenth a. M. 11, r.h., note 1, dotted sixteenth.

[15] Corrant

SOURCE: Ed. 1707, p. 16, "Corrant"

(Cf. [56a] Courante)

M. 1, b, note 1, half-note. M. 2, b, note 1, half-note. M. 6, r.h., final quarter beat, rest is sixteenth. Mm. 6 and 7, a, beat 1, eighth- and two quarter-rests vertically aligned. M. 11, t, rest 2, sixteenth. Mm. 15 and 16, a, beat 1, four quarter-rests vertically aligned; t, note 1, half-note.

[16] Saraband

SOURCE: Ed. 1707, p. 17, "Saraband"

M. 6, b, half-note. M. 14, a, note 1, dotted quarter-note.

[17] Aire

SOURCE: Ed. 1707, p. 18, "Aire"

M. 1, b, note 1, dotted half-note.

[18] Jigg

SOURCE: Ed. 1707, p. 19, "Iigg"

M. 11, b, half-note. M. 31, b, half-note. M. 33, b, half-note c, quarter-note c, quarter-note d. M. 41, b, half-note. M. 42, double-bar at end of measure indicating repeat, but repeat clearly begins after the following measure.

[19] Prelude

SOURCE: Ed. 1707, p. 20, "Prelude"

[20] Allmand

SOURCE: Ed. 1707, p. 21, "Allmand"

M. 1, r.h., beat 1, middle note of chord is f'-sharp. M. 7, l.h., note 2, d. M. 11, a, note 1, contemporary hand has added tie from previous measure. Mm. 12 and 13, s, note 1, whole-note. M. 14, b, note 2, half-note. M. 19, a, beat 1, additional quarter-rest. M. 20, b, beat 4, contemporary hand has added a quarter-rest under the f-sharp. M. 25, b, note 2, quarter-note by contemporary hand. Mm. 25 and 26, s, note 1, whole-note.

[21] Corrant

SOURCE: Ed. 1707, p. 22, "Corrant"

M. 1, t, note 3, half-note. M. 3, a, note 1, c'-sharp. M. 4, s, note 7, half-note. Mm. 7 and 8, b, note 1, half-note. M. 13, t, note 2, half-note. M. 14, b, note 1, half-note.

[22] Saraband

SOURCE: Ed. 1707, p. 23, "Saraband" "Slow"

M. 1, b, note 1, half-note. M. 3, t, note 1, half-note. M. 11, t, note 1, half-note. M. 16, b, note 2, quarter-note. M. 20, l.h., note 4, undotted eighth-note.

[23] Jigg

SOURCE: Ed. 1707, p. 24, "Iigg"

M. 4, l.h., beat 3, lower note, e-sharp. M. 21, l.h., note 1, b corrected to a by contemporary hand.

[24] Round O

SOURCE: Ed. 1707, p. 25, "Round O"

M. 13, l.h., note 2, d.

[25] Prelude

SOURCE: Ed. 1707, p. 26, "Prelude"

M. 1, r.h., beat 3, d′ is dotted half-note tied to following measure.

[26] Allmand

PRINCIPAL SOURCE: Ed. 1707, p. 26, "Allmand"

OTHER SOURCES: (1) Lbl 1, fol. 10r, "Almand"/"Dr. Blow"; (2) Och 2, fol. 19Av; (3) Bc, p. 129. "Allmand"/"Dr. Blow"

Lbl 1, Och 2 and Bc have similar readings, differing from Ed. 1707 mainly in melodic variants and left-hand texture. The presence of the piece in Bc indicates that it was written no later than 1687.

M. 9, r.h., note 1, ornament over note 2. M. 11, r.h., note 12, c″. M. 13, r.h., note 10, f′.

[27] Corrant

PRINCIPAL SOURCE: Ed. 1707, p. 27, "Corrant"

SECONDARY SOURCE: Wc, p. 102, "Corant"

Upbeat, l.h., rest in Ed. 1707 only. M. 1, b, note 2, tie in Ed. 1707 only. M. 2, t, beat 1, dot on last note of previous measure instead of rest in Wc. M. 4, r.h., note 1, ornament in Ed. 1707 only. M. 6, s, note 1, half-note in Ed. 1707. Mm. 6 and 7, l.h., last eighth beat, rest in Ed. 1707 only. M. 10, r.h., note 1, ornament in Ed. 1707 only. M. 11, t, note 2, sharp in Wc, note 6 in Ed. 1707 only. M. 12, r.h., note 1, ornament in Ed. 1707 only. M. 13, r.h., note 1, ornament inflection is editorial. M. 14, s, note 5, sharp in Wc. M. 15, s, note 1, half-note in Ed. 1707; a, note 3, tie in Wc; l.h., last eighth beat, rest in Ed. 1707 only.

[28] Saraband

SOURCE: Ed. 1707, p. 27, "Saraband"

M. 3, t, beat 1, eighth-rest. M. 10, b, half-note. M. 16, s, half-note.

[29] Bore

SOURCE: Ed. 1707, p. 28, "Bore"

Mm. 4 and 5, l.h., note 2, half-note. M. 13, b, note 1, half-note.

[30] Aire

SOURCE: Ed. 1707, p. 28, "Aire"

M. 10, r.h., note 3, d″. M. 13, l.h., dotted whole-note. M. 14, r.h., note 3, sic. The player may wish to flat

m. 14, l.h., note 2; m. 15, l.h., note 2; and m. 16, r.h., notes 1 and 5. M. 25, l.h., note 3, a. M. 27, t, half-note. M. 30, s and t, quarter-notes (bass note stems point up).

[31] Minuet

SOURCE: Ed. 1707, p. 29, "Minuet"

M. 8, b, half-note.

[32] Prelude

SOURCE: Ed. 1707, p. 30, "Prelude"

[33] Allmand

SOURCE: Ed. 1707, pp. 30–31, "Allmand"

M. 4, r.h., rest is sixteenth. M. 8, r.h., note 7, c″-sharp. M. 15, b, notes 2 and 3, e and f corrected to g and a by contemporary hand. M. 19, b, notes 9 and 10, d and f corrected to f and a by contemporary hand. M. 20, t, note 1, b-flat; b, note 1, d.

[34] Aire

SOURCE: Ed. 1707, p. 32, "Aire"

[35] Jigg

SOURCE: Ed. 1707, p. 33, "Jigg"

M. 24, b, note 1, quarter-note. M. 28, r.h., second half of measure, c″, a, c″.

[36] The Dream

SOURCE: Ed. 1707, p. 34, "The Dream"

M. 2, b, note 1, quarter-note.

[37] Minuet

SOURCE: Ed. 1707, p. 35, "Minuet"

M. 8, r.h., lower note, half-note (upper note stem up). M. 24, s, half-note; a, note 2, quarter-note.

[38] Toccata

SOURCE: Wc, pp. 25–30, "Toccata Dell Sign^re Baptist Draghi Terzi Minore"

M. 3, a, beat 3, placed on second half of beat 2. M. 5, a, last 4 notes, e′-flat, e′-flat, f′, e′-flat. M. 20, a, rest is eighth. M. 28, a, beat 2, notes are a′, b′-flat, a′. M. 39, t, beat 2, sic. The b-flats are needed to complete the second-inversion triad, which is why the fugal subject does not begin here in the usual way, i.e., with g, a. The editorial f-sharp on beat 3 makes for awkward voice-leading, but it is nevertheless implied by the harmony. A suggested alternative is to substitute g for the second b-flat. M. 41, l.h., note 10, d′. M. 46, a, note 12, quarter-note, but placed as if it were an eighth. M. 47, s, note 2, sixteenth-note, note 7, eighth tied to sixteenth-note. M. 50, a, beat 3, c' and f' are quarter-notes, resulting in too many beats in the measure. As eighth-notes, they produce consecutive octaves with the tenor.

[39] Trumpet

SOURCE: Wc, pp. 37–48, "Trumpet D'ell Sign^re Baptist D Terza Majare"

M. 1, l.h., C-sharp. M. 31, r.h., note 6, undotted eighth-note. M. 40, t, beat 3, note is quarter-note. M. 46, l.h., last note, b. M. 62, r.h., notes 10–12 and 14–16, two thirty-seconds followed by sixteenth. M. 64, l.h., note 1, f-sharp. M. 118, l.h., F-sharp. M. 123, l.h., note 1, F-sharp. M. 132, entire left hand a third higher. M. 156, r.h., beat 1, first rest is sixteenth.

[40] Ayre

SOURCE: Wc, pp. 71–73, "Ayre"

M. 9, r.h., notes 3 and 4, quarter-notes. M. 15, entire l.h. a third higher. M. 18, r.h., note 1 is e'–g' interval.

[41] Prelude

SOURCE: Wc, p. 74, "Sute of Lesson Dell J Bap Draghi" "Prelude"

M. 5, r.h., note 15, b'-flat. M. 7, t, note 3, f', note 7, c'-natural.

[42] Allemande

SOURCE: Wc, pp. 75–77, "Allemande"

M. 8, s, notes 1 and 2, sixteenth-notes; t, note 2, sixteenth-note; b, note 3, eighth-note. M. 17, s, note 4, sixteenth-note. M. 19, r.h., notes 1–6 are double the time values. M. 20, r.h., notes 2–4, 9–11, 13, and 14 are double the time values, note 9, f''-natural. M. 22, r.h., notes 2 and 3 are sixteenth-notes. M. 24, r.h., note 9, dotted sixteenth-note.

[43] Arieta

SOURCE: Wc, pp. 78–79, "Arieta"

M. 12, b, note 2, c.

[44] [Bouree]

SOURCE: Wc, pp. 80–81

M. 8, s, notes 3 and 4, quarter-notes. M. 33, r.h., note 4, b'-natural.

[45] Prelud[e]

SOURCES: (1) Wc, p. 82, "Prelud"; (2) Ob, pp. 20–21

M. 13, in Ob, s, last eighth beat, dotted eighth-note fol-

lowed by two thirty-second-notes; a, last eighth beat, quarter-note. M. 16, in Wc, l.h., note 6, E-flat.

[46] Alemande

PRINCIPAL SOURCE: Wc, pp. 83–85, "Alemande"

OTHER SOURCE: Ob, pp. 22–25

The ordering of the C-minor group in Wc has been preserved because it contains eight pieces, whereas Ob has only three. Wc is therefore the principal source for the sake of consistency (but see note for [52] [Saraband]). Ob has more ornaments and generally thicker textures, but few melodic variants.

M. 8, t, note 2, f. M. 10, r.h., note 9, g'-sharp. M. 20, s, note 8, upper note is a'-natural. M. 22, b, last eighth-note, e-flat. A whole-note c for the left hand appears after the final measure.

[47] Slow

SOURCE: Wc, pp. 86–87, "Slow"

[48] Roundeaue

SOURCE: Wc, pp. 88–89, "Roundeaue"

M. 4, a, last note, quarter-note. M. 10, r.h., beat 4, b'-flats. M. 19, r.h., beat 3, two quarter-notes. M. 20, a, last note, quarter-note.

[49] Aire

PRINCIPAL SOURCE: Wc, pp. 90–92, "Aire"

OTHER SOURCE: Ob, pp. 26–28

Ob does not contain the "petite reprise" from m. 26 to the end.

M. 15, r.h., note 2, e'-flat. M. 18, r.h., note 5, g''-flat. M. 22, l.h., note 3, d-sharp. M. 25, r.h., note 1, quarter-note. M. 28, r.h., note 6, a'-natural.

[50] [Aire]

SOURCE: Wc, pp. 93–95

M. 7, b, beat 4, AA. M. 18, a, beat 4, c''-flat. M. 24, t, note 4, e'-flat.

[51] [Aire]

SOURCE: Wc, pp. 96–97

[52] [Saraband]

PRINCIPAL SOURCE: Cfm 1, fols. 1r-1v, ":B" (at end)

SECONDARY SOURCE: Wc, pp. 98–99

The piece is placed as in Wc in order to complete the C-minor group, even though Cfm 1 is the principal source.

M. 1, r.h., note 1, ornament in Cfm 1 only (inflection editorial). M. 2, r.h., notes 1 and 3, ornaments in Cfm 1 only; t, note 1, quarter-note in Wc; b, beat 2, dotted quarter-note followed by eighth-note in Wc, note 5, ornament in Cfm 1 only. M. 4, l.h. beat 2, dotted quarter-note followed by eighth-note in Wc. M. 5, r.h., note 5, ornament in Cfm 1 only. M. 6, r.h., note 1, ornament in Cfm 1 only, dotted half-note (no rest) in Wc. M. 7, r.h., note 3, ornament in Cfm 1 only; b, note 1, A-natural in Wc. M. 8, t, quarter-rest followed by dotted whole-note in Cfm 1, half-rest followed by whole-note in Wc; b, whole-note G followed by half-note A-flat in Wc. M. 9, s, notes 1 and 3, ornaments in Cfm 1 only; a, note 1, in Wc, note 2, dotted half-note in Wc; t, note 1, in Cfm 1 only. M. 10, r.h., ornament in Cfm 1 only; l.h., beat 1, dotted quarter-note followed by eighth-note in Wc, note 2, c in Cfm 1, note 5, ornament in Cfm 1 only. M. 13, t, note 1, in Cfm 1 only. M. 15, l.h., note 3, ornament in Cfm 1 only. M. 16, l.h., beat 2, upper note in Wc. M. 17, r.h., note 5, ornament in Cfm 1 only. M. 18, r.h., note 5, ornament in Cfm 1 only. M. 20, r.h., note 1, ornament in Cfm 1 only; t, note 2, b-flat in Wc. M. 21, r.h., note 1, ornament in Cfm 1 only, beat 3, two quarter-notes in Wc. M. 22, r.h., note 3, ornament in Cfm 1 only; l.h., beat 1, middle note a-natural in Wc. M. 23, r.h., note 5, ornament in Cfm 1 only; l.h., beat 1, chord is third higher in Wc. M. 24, l.h., beat 1, dotted quarter-note followed by eighth-note in Wc, note 5, ornament in Cfm 1 only. M. 25, in Wc (rest is editorial).

[53] Almond

SOURCE: Wc, pp. 100–101, "Almond" "4 Süet Comp.ᵈ by Senʳ J. Bapᵗ Draghi"

In Wc this piece is followed by [27] Corrant and [64] Saraband.

M. 4, a, beat 2, quarter-note tied to another quarter-note on beat 4. M. 27, l.h., beat 3, half-notes.

[54] Prelude

SOURCE: U, p. 64. "Sute of Lessons d'ell Signᵗ Baptist Draghi" "Prelude"

(Cf. [1] Prelude)

[55] [Allemande]

PRINCIPAL SOURCE: Cfm 1, fols. 3v–4r, "B" "Saturday Feb: ye 7th 1701/2" (at end)

SECONDARY SOURCE: U, pp. 65–67, "Allemande"

Nos. [54] through [58] are presented in the same order as in U, even though Cfm 1 is the principal source for this piece and for [57]. (See also under [52] [Saraband].) The order of pieces in Cfm 1 is as follows: [52], [59], [60], [57], [61].

Key signature of two flats in U.

M. 1, l.h., note 3, e'-flat in U. M. 2, l.h., note 2, tie in Cfm 1 only, note 4, ornament in Cfm 1 only, beat 4, dotted eighth- and sixteenth-notes in U. M. 3, l.h., note 4, ornament in Cfm 1 only, beat 4, dotted eighth- and sixteenth-notes in U. M. 4, r.h., beats 2 and 4, dotted eighth- and sixteenth-note pairs in U. M. 5, t, note 4, or-

nament in Cfm 1 only, beat 4, dotted eighth- and sixteenth-notes in U. M. 6, r.h., beats 2 and 4, dotted eighth- and sixteenth-note pairs in U, note 4, e"-flat in U; l.h., beat 2, dotted eighth- and sixteenth-notes in U. M. 7, r.h., beat 4, dotted eighth- and sixteenth-notes in U. M. 8, l.h., beats 1, 2 and 4, dotted eighth- and sixteenth-note pairs in U. M. 9, r.h., beat 4, dotted eighth- and sixteenth-notes in U. M. 10, r.h., beat 3, dotted eighth- and two thirty-second-notes in U; t, note 2, in Cfm 1 only. M. 11, r.h., notes 4–6, two thirty-seconds followed by a sixteenth in Cfm 1, three thirty-second-notes in U, beat 3, written-out turn in U; l.h., beat 3, eighth-rest followed by eighth-note in U. M. 12, l.h., beat 4, ornament in Cfm 1 only. M. 14, r.h., note 4, ornament in Cfm 1 only. M. 17, l.h., beat 2, lower voice is c–f eighth-notes in U; t, beat 3, eighth-rest followed by eighth-note in U. M. 18, r.h., note 1, ornament in Cfm 1 only, beats 1 and 2, quarter-note c" tied to sixteenth-note c" followed by d", c", b'-flat sixteenth-notes in U, note 3, ornament in Cfm 1 only, beat 3, dotted eighth- and sixteenth-notes in U. M. 20, t, beat 4, in U; b, beat 4, d', b-flat eighth-notes in U, f in Cfm 1 only. M. 21, r.h., note 7, d", d' thirty-second-notes in U. M. 22, r.h., notes 2 and 3, sixteenth-notes in Cfm 1, note 7, ornament in Cfm 1 only. M. 23, t, beats 2 and 3, in U, beat 4, eighth-rest followed by eighth-note in U; b, beat 2, one quarter-note B in U. M. 24, r.h., notes 1 and 3, ornaments in Cfm 1 only. M. 25, r.h., notes 6–8, two thirty-seconds followed by a sixteenth in Cfm 1, three sixty-fourth-notes in U. M. 26, r.h., beat 4, two eighth-notes in U; b, beat 4, dotted eighth-note e followed by sixteenth-note d in U. M. 27, r.h., beat 1, two eighth-notes in U; t, beat 2, eighth-rest followed by eighth-note c' in U; b, beat 1, dotted eighth-note e-flat followed by sixteenth-note f in U; l.h., beat 3, lowest voice is f, g eighth-notes in U, beat 4, middle note of chord in U. M. 29, r.h., note 2, e', d' thirty-second-notes in U, beat 3, quarter-note a' with forefall in U, beat 4, dotted eighth-note g with shake followed by sixteenth-note f'-sharp in U; l.h., beat 3, d', c eighth-notes in U, beat 4, U has quarter-note d in tenor, eighth-rest followed by eighth-note D in bass. M. 30, r.h., beat 1, two eighth-notes in U, note 3, ornament in Cfm 1 only.

[56a] Courante
[56b] Double of the Courante

SOURCE: U, pp. 68–71, "Courante" "Double of ye: Courante"

(Cf. [15] Corrant)

Double: Mm. 6 and 7, s, note 1, undotted half-note. Mm. 15 and 16, s, note 1, undotted half-note.

[57] [Arietta]

PRINCIPAL SOURCE: Cfm 1, fols. 4v–5r, ":B:" "Saturday Feb: ye 7th: 1701/2:" (at end)

SECONDARY SOURCE: U, pp. 71–73, "Arietta"

Key signature of two flats in U.

M. 3, r.h., note 2, ornament in Cfm 1 only. M. 4, r.h.,

note 1, e″-flat in U.   M. 8, r.h., beat 2, quarter-note (no rest) in U; l.h., beat 3, quarter-note (no rest) in U.   M. 10, t, note 1 (and tie), in U; b, beat 3, dotted quarter-note in Cfm 1.   M. 11, r.h., beat 3, ornament written out in U.   M. 15, r.h., note 2, tie in Cfm 1 only.   M. 16, b, beats 3 and 4, quarter-notes in U.   M. 17, r.h., note 7, ornament in Cfm 1 only.   M. 18, r.h., beat 1, e″, g″, f″, e″ sixteenth-notes in U.   M. 19, l.h., note 1, upper note is dotted quarter followed by eighth-rest in U, beat 2, quarter-note (no rest) in U, beat 4, ornament in Cfm 1 only.   M. 20, r.h., note 4, ornament in Cfm 1 only.   M. 21, r.h., notes 7 and 11, ornaments in Cfm 1 only.   M. 22, "petite reprise" indication in Cfm 1 only; l.h., notes 3 and 6, ornaments in Cfm 1 only.   M. 23, l.h., note 2, ornament in Cfm 1 only.   Mm. 25 and 29, r.h., note 1, ornament in Cfm 1 only.

[58] Gigue

SOURCE: U, pp. 74–75, "Gigue"/"By J: B: D:"

M. 5, b, note 1, undotted half-note.   M. 27, a, note 1, undotted half-note.

[59] [Aire]

SOURCE: Cfm 1, fols. 1v–2v, "B" (at end)

M. 8, l.h., note 3, B.

[60] Almond

SOURCE: Cfm 1, fols. 2v–3r, "Almond:"/"B"

Mm. 17 and 18, r.h., chord is half-note.

[61] Almand

SOURCE: Cfm 1, fols. 5v–7r, "Almand"/"B" "Thursday Feb ye 13th: 1701/2 allmost 2 a Clock"

M. 5, l.h., note 6, ornament sic (English "shake" sign).   M. 6, t, note 1, quarter-note.   M. 7, b, beat 3, quarter-note.   M. 8, r.h., note 6, eighth-note.   M. 9, r.h., last two notes, thirty-seconds.   M. 25, t, beat 4, rest is eighth.   M. 26, t, note 4, dotted sixteenth-note.   M. 29, s, note 11, eighth-note.

[62] Almaine

PRINCIPAL SOURCE: Och 2, fols. 1Av–2Ar, "Almaine"

SECONDARY SOURCE: Och 1, fol. 1Av

Och 1 has only this piece and the first few measures of the following Corant, and they appear to have been copied from Och 2.

M. 1, r.h., last note, sixty-fourth-note in Och 1; l.h., ties in Och 2 only.   M. 3, r.h., beats 2 and 4, ornaments in Och 2 only; b, beat 2, added f in Och 1.   M. 4, r.h., note 9, ornament in Och 2 only.   M. 8, r.h., beat 3, slur in Och 2 only, beat 4, ornament in Och 2 only; t, note 1, half-note on beat 1 in Och 1.   M. 12, r.h., note 3, ornament in Och 2 only, note 6, backfall in Och 2 (no ornament in Och 1).   M. 13, r.h., note 3, ornament in Och 2 only; b, note 2,

in Och 1.   M. 14, t, note 4, ornament in Och 2 only.   M. 15, r.h., last note, a′ Och 1.   M. 22, t, beat 2, tie in Och 1, beat 3, half-note in both sources; b, beat 2, half-note in both sources, beat 3, rest in Och 2 only, dotted quarter-note in both sources.

[63] Corant

PRINCIPAL SOURCE: Och 2, fol. 2Av, "Corant"

SECONDARY SOURCE: Och 1, fol. 2Ar (first four measures and right hand of measures 5 and 6 only)

Time signature in Och 2 only.
Upbeat, l.h., rest in Och 1.   M. 15, b, half-note.   Mm. 16 and 17, entire chord is dotted half.   M. 35, entire chord is dotted half.

[64] Saraband

PRINCIPAL SOURCE: Wc, pp. 103–5, "Saraband"

OTHER SOURCE: Och 2, fol. 3Ar, "Sarabant"/"Senꞈ Baptiṣṭ" (first 24 measures only)

The piece is presented here to complete the D-minor group as in Och 2, even though Wc, with the added variations, is the principal source. In general, the middle voice in Och 2 is in the tenor, rather than in the alto, resulting in lower-lying textures. Its version is melodically rather less refined. It also indicates a "petite reprise" from m. 17.
M. 28, r.h., note 4, e″.   M. 47, s, note 2, c″.   M. 55, l.h., beat 3, upper note is c′.

[65] [Prelude]

PRINCIPAL SOURCE: LAuc, pp. 2–4

SECONDARY SOURCE: Lbl 3, p. 24, "5ᵐᵉ Suitte en B mineur" "Pieces de Mr. Baptiste" "Prelude"

Lbl 3 contains this and all of the following pieces in B minor, and its order of pieces is retained.
M. 4, r.h., tie in LAuc only.   M. 5, a, note 6, ornament in LAuc only.   M. 6, t, beat 2, dotted quarter-notes in both sources.   M. 8, s, note 1, eighth-note in Lbl 3; a, note 2, tie in LAuc only.   M. 9, t, beat 1, rest is two sixteenths in LAuc.   M. 11, t, note 4, ornament in LAuc only.   M. 12, a, note 1, in LAuc only.   M. 13, b, note 4, tie in Lbl 3.

[66] [Allemande]

PRINCIPAL SOURCE: LAuc, pp. 14–17

SECONDARY SOURCE: Lbl 3, pp. 24–25, "Allemande"

All dashed ties are by authority of Lbl 3.
M. 5, r.h., beat 4, ornament in LAuc only.   M. 6, s, note 5, ornament in LAuc only.   M. 7, r.h., note 1, ornament in LAuc only.   M. 9, a, note 1, in LAuc only.   M. 12, s, note 1, ornament in LAuc only.   M. 16, b, note 1, in Lbl 3 note is tied from beat 1 of the previous measure, even though the f-sharp in the previous measure is a half-note.   M. 20, l.h., note 3, A in both sources.   M. 22, r.h.,

note 1, a'-natural in Lbl 3.   M. 26, l.h., note 2, natural in Lbl 3.   M. 27, s, note 5, ornament in LAuc only.   M. 31, a, note 2, in LAuc only.   M. 33, s, note 8, g"-natural in both sources; t, note 1, dotted eighth-note in Lbl 3.   M. 34, s, beat 3, first note is b'-sharp in both sources; a, beat 3, in LAuc only. The sharp in the soprano is actually meant for the alto g', but is placed a little too high in LAuc. This provides circumstantial evidence that the scribe of Lbl 3 was copying from LAuc, inadvertently leaving out the alto g' and assigning the sharp to the wrong note.   M. 41, r.h., note 4, ornament in LAuc only.   M. 51, in Lbl 3.

[67]   [Courante]

PRINCIPAL SOURCE: LAuc, pp. 12–13

SECONDARY SOURCE: Lbl 3, p. 26, "Courante"

Time signature 3/2 in Lbl 3.

M. 3, s, note 2, ornament in LAuc only; a, note 1, half-note in LAuc.   M. 4, s, note 1, half-note in Lbl 3; a, note 1, quarter-note in both sources. In LAuc, the following c'-sharp is placed within the measure as if the d' were an eighth-note. Lbl 3 has the c'-sharp on the fourth quarter beat.   M. 5, b, note 3, ornament in LAuc only.   Mm. 6 and 7, s, note 1, half-note in both sources; r.h., fourth quarter beat, all notes of the chord tied in LAuc; l.h., fourth quarter beat, upper note is f-sharp in both sources, despite a tie from the previous note d in LAuc only.   M. 8, b, note 1, half-note in Lbl 3; l.h., sixth quarter beat, ornament for g-sharp in LAuc only.   M. 9, t, note 4, half-note in Lbl 3.   M. 13, t, rest and first two notes, in LAuc only.   M. 14, b, note 1, half-note in Lbl 3.   M. 15, b, note 1, half-note in Lbl 3.

[68]   [Tombeau]

PRINCIPAL SOURCE: LAuc, pp. 18–19

SECONDARY SOURCE: Lbl 3, pp. 26–27, "Tombeau"

M. 4, a, note 1, in LAuc only.   M. 8, s, note 1, half-note in Lbl 3.   M. 10, b, note 1, half-note in LAuc.   M. 11, a, beat 2, in LAuc only.   M. 13, a, half-note in Lbl 3.   M. 16, a, note 1, in LAuc only.   M. 17, a, note 1, half-note in LAuc.   M. 18, t, half-note in Lbl 3.   M. 22, s, note 3, dotted quarter-note in LAuc.   M. 24, s, note 1, half-note in both sources.

[69]   Gigue

PRINCIPAL SOURCE: Lbl 3, p. 27, "Gigue"

SECONDARY SOURCE: T, fols. 27v–28r, "Gigue en B mineur"

Time signature 6/4 in T—all note values doubled.

M. 3, s, note 1, ornament in Lbl 3 only.   M. 4, a, beat 5, in Lbl 3 only.   M. 7, l.h., note 1, ornament in Lbl 3 only.   M. 20, b, note 1, quarter-note (i.e., half-note in 6/4) in T.   M. 24, l.h., note 1, tie in T.   M. 25, r.h., note 4, ornament in Lbl 3 only.   M. 26, r.h., beat 4, middle note of chord is e' in T; t, note 2, quarter-note in Lbl 3, tie in T.   M. 30, r.h., beat 4, tie in Lbl 3 only.   M. 31, b, beat 4,

dotted quarter-note (no eighth-rest) in Lbl 3.   M. 34, s, note 1, quarter-note in Lbl 3.   M. 39, r.h., notes 1 and 2, sixteenth-notes in Lbl 3.   M. 40, r.h., note 4, ornament in Lbl 3 only.   M. 41, t and b, beat 4, quarter-notes in Lbl 3.

[70]   Allemande

PRINCIPAL SOURCES: (1) Lbl 3, p. 28, "Allemande"; (2) Cfm 2, p. 58, "Almand"

OTHER SOURCE: Lbl 4, fols. 29v–30r, "Almand"

Lbl 4 has a text similar to Cfm 2, but it generally suppresses the dotted sixteenth/thirty-second-note groupings in favor of equal sixteenths.

M. 1, in Cfm 2, r.h., beat 2, first e" is eighth-note, ornament is "shake turned."   M. 2, in Cfm 2, r.h., beat 1, upper note is dotted quarter.   M. 3, in Cfm 2, l.h., note 1, g'-flat (the flat probably intended to cancel the sharp in the previous measure).   M. 4, in Lbl 3, b, beat 3, quarter-rest.   M. 5, in Lbl 3, b, note 2, quarter-note.   M. 7, in Cfm 2, t, note 1, quarter-note.   M. 8, in Cfm 2, a, beat 3, quarter-note.   Mm. 11 and 12, in Lbl 3, r.h., beat 3, lowest note of chord is f'-sharp.   M. 18, in Cfm 2, a, beat 2, the two g's are a dotted sixteenth followed by a thirty-second.   M. 19, in Lbl 3, t, note 4, dotted quarter-note.

[71]   Rondeau

PRINCIPAL SOURCE: Lbl 3, pp. 28–29, "Rondeau"

OTHER SOURCE: Cfm 2, p. 59

M. 6, t, half-note.

[72]   [Autre Rondeau]

PRINCIPAL SOURCE: LAuc, pp. 20–21

SECONDARY SOURCE: Lbl 3, p. 29, "Autre Rondeau"

M. 4, s, note 8, ornament in LAuc only; a, in LAuc only.   M. 5, s, notes 1 and 5, ornaments in LAuc only. At the end of each *couplet,* both sources normally give only the first two beats of the refrain to indicate the repeat, meaning a return to beat 3 of the refrain. (The sign 𝄋 is used in Lbl 3 only.) In this measure, however, LAuc includes the third beat of the refrain, presumably to indicate the added shake on the d" of beat 3.   M. 7, r.h., note 3, ornaments in LAuc only; s and a, beat 4, a third higher in LAuc.   M. 8, t, last note is a-sharp in Lbl 3.   M. 9, s, note 13, ornament in LAuc only.

[73]   [Allemande]

PRINCIPAL SOURCE: LAuc, pp. 4–11

SECONDARY SOURCE: Lbl 3, pp. 30–31

M. 2, a, beat 2, in LAuc only.   M. 3, s, beat 4, forefall in Lbl 3.   M. 4, l.h., note 9, ornament in LAuc only.   M. 6, l.h., note 8, ornament in LAuc only.   M. 8, a, beat 1, tie in Lbl 3.   M. 9, b, note 1, half-note in both sources, beat 2, rest in Lbl 3, note is D in both sources.   M. 10, s, note 1, ornament in LAuc only, note 4, quarter-note in Lbl 3; l.h., beat 2, dotted sixteenths and thirty-seconds in

Lbl 3. M. 12, l.h., note 7, ornament in LAuc only. M. 13, s, note 6, ornament in LAuc only. M. 14, r.h., note 2, ornament in LAuc only. M. 16, t, note 4, a-natural in Lbl 3. M. 19, s, note 4, sixteenth-note in both sources (preceded by sixteenth-rest in Lbl 3). M. 20, b, beat 3, d in Lbl 3. M. 21, s, notes 3 and 8, ornaments in LAuc only; a, note 4, ornament in LAuc only. M. 24, s, beat 4, ornament on g" in LAuc only. M. 31, l.h., notes 1 and 2, dotted eighth followed by sixteenth in Lbl 3. M. 32, s, beat 3, ornament in LAuc only. M. 33, s, note 1, tie in LAuc only. M. 35, a, note 1, eighth-note in both sources. M. 41, r.h., note 6, ornament in LAuc only; t, note 1, tie in LAuc only, note 2, ornament in LAuc only. M. 44, r.h., note 6, ornament in LAuc only, note 7, g'-natural in Lbl 3. M. 45, t, note 1, quarter-note in Lbl 3, note 2, a in both sources. M. 50, s, note 11, tie in LAuc only. M. 52, s, note 11, tie in LAuc only; a, note 3, dotted eighth-note in both sources; t, note 1, quarter-note in both sources; b, note 5, tie in LAuc only. M. 53, a, note 2, in LAuc only; t, note 3, ornament in LAuc only. M. 54, s, note 7, tie in LAuc only; a, note 2, dotted eighth-note in both sources. M. 56, a, note 1, in LAuc only. M. 57, r.h., beat 4, ornament in LAuc only.

[74] Prelude

SOURCE: Lbl 5, p. 51, "Prelude: by Mr Baptist"

M. 4, r.h., notes 14 and 16, sixteenth-notes. M. 5, r.h., note 11, thirty-second-note.

[75] Almand

SOURCE: Lbl 5, pp. 51–53, "Almand"

M. 8, b, beat 4, A is quarter-note but placed as an eighth-note. M. 15, r.h., beat 4, last two notes are thirty-seconds. M. 17, s, note 1, eighth-note. M. 25, r.h., note 6, eighth-note. M. 26, r.h., note 3, sixteenth-note.

[76] Saraband

SOURCE: Lbl 5, pp. 54–55, "Saraband"

M. 18, r.h., note 2, eighth-note. M. 25, r.h., note 8, eighth-note.

[77] [Aire]

SOURCE: Lbl 5, pp. 55–57, "by Mr. Baptist" "brisk"

[78] [Aire]

SOURCE: Lbl 5, pp. 57–58

M. 12, r.h., note 2, dotted sixteenth-note, note 6, eighth-note.

[79] Gavotte

SOURCE: CDp, fols. 23Ar–23Av, "Gavotte"/"Baptist"

M. 15, b, note 3, a. M. 16, t, beat 3, f.

[80] Slow Minuet

SOURCE: CDp, fols. 23Av–24Ar, "Slow Minuet"/ "Baptist"

M. 13, t, undotted half-note.

[81] [Almand]

SOURCE: CDp, fol. 24Ar–24Av

M. 10, r.h., beat 3, chord is third higher. M. 11, r.h., beat 4, eighth-rest before final note. M. 18, l.h., note 2, d-sharp, not preceded by rest.

[82] Tune

SOURCE: En, fol. 11v, "Tune"/"Senᴵ Baptist"

M. 2, l.h., beat 1, lower note is e.

[83] Tune

SOURCE: En, fol. 12r, "Tune"/"Senᴵ Baptist"

[84] A Ground

SOURCE: En, fols. 33v–35r, "A Ground"/"Senior Baptistˢ Ground"

[85] Italian air

SOURCE: Lbl 2, fol. 7v, "Ital: air"/"Sᴵ Bap:"

Acknowledgments

It is my pleasure to acknowledge the courteous assistance offered me by the staffs of all libraries in which materials for this project were consulted. For permission to publish these transcriptions and facsimiles, I wish to thank the British Library; the Curators of the Bodleian Library, Oxford; the Governing Body of Christ Church, Oxford; the Syndics of the Fitzwilliam Museum, Cambridge; the County of South Glamorgan Libraries; the Trustees of the National Library of Scotland; the Library of Congress, Washington; the Library of the University of Illinois at Urbana-Champaign; the Library of the School of Music at Yale University, New Haven; and the William Andrews Clark Memorial Library, University of California, Los Angeles. I am indebted to James Coover, Head of the Music Library at SUNY/Buffalo for his indulgence in obtaining materials on my behalf, to Dr. Watkins Shaw for kindly pointing out two concordances that had escaped my notice, to Alexander Silbiger for bringing the Urbana source to my attention, and in particular to David Fuller and Bruce Gustafson for their expert advice during the early stages of this project. Finally, I wish to express my gratitude to the publishers of this series for their confidence and encouragement.

Notes

1. See *New Grove Dictionary of Music and Musicians*, s.v., "Draghi, Antonio," by Rudolf Schnitzler; and s.v. "Draghi, Giovanni Battista," by Ian Spink.

2. John Wilson, ed., *Roger North on Music* (London: Novello, 1959), 301–2. See also p. 348.

3. London, British Library, MS Add. 15897. Quoted in Wilibald Nagel, "Annalen der englischen Hofmusik," *Monatshefte für Musikgeschichte* 26 (1894): Beilagen, 52n.

4. J. C. M. Weale, ed., *Registers of the Catholic Chapels Royal and of the Portuguese Embassy Chapel, 1662–1829*, Marriages, no. 178 (London: Catholic Record Society, 1941). Quoted in Rosamund Harding, *A Thematic Catalogue of the Works of Matthew Locke* (Oxford: Alden Press, 1971), xxix.

5. F. H. Blackburne, ed., *Calendar of State Papers*, Domestic Series (London: His Majesty's Stationery Office, 1915; Liechtenstein: Kraus Reprints, 1968), 21:284.

6. London, British Library, MS Harleian 7338. Quoted in Sir John Hawkins, *A General History of the Science and Practice of Music* (1875 ed.; reprint, Graz: Akademische Druck- u. Verlagsanstalt, 1969), 2:691.

7. Hawkins, *General History*, 2:718.

8. *A Collection of Improvement of Husbandry and Trade* 6 (22 February 1694/5). Quoted in Michael Tilmouth, "The Royal Academies of 1695," *Music and Letters* 38 (1957): 327.

9. William van Lennep, Emmett L. Avery, et al., eds., *The London Stage, 1660–1800* (Carbondale, Ill.: Southern Illinois University Press, 1960–68), pt. 1:493; pt. 2:9.

10. William A. Shaw, ed., *Calendar of Treasury Books* (London: His Majesty's Stationery Office, 1950), 22:336.

11. London, British Library, MS Add. 33287; London, Royal College of Music, MS 1106; Tenbury, St. Michael's College, MS 1226. For a discussion of the work, see Ernest Brennecke, Jr., "Dryden's Odes and Draghi's Music," *Publications of the Modern Language Association* 49 (1934): 1–36.

12. One harpsichord piece ([26] Allmand) appears in J. A. Fuller Maitland, ed., *The Contemporaries of Purcell* (London: J. & W. Chester, 1921), 2:12, as a work of Blow.

13. Reprinted in Bernardo Pasquini, *Collected Works for Keyboard*, ed. Maurice Brooks Haynes, Corpus of Early Keyboard Music, vol. 5, pt. 6 (Rome: American Institute of Musicology, 1968), 41.

14. In this connection see also Bruce Gustafson, "A Letter from Mr. Lebègue Concerning his Preludes," *Recherches sur la musique française classique* 17 (1977): 7–14.

15. Blow's ground is transcribed in Fuller Maitland, ed., *Contemporaries*, 1:18; and in Thurston Dart, ed., *The Second Part of Musick's Hand-maid*, Early Keyboard Music, K10, 2d rev. ed. (London: Stainer and Bell, 1969), no. 23.

16. General information on some of these sources, and on English keyboard sources of the period, can be found in John Caldwell, *English Keyboard Music before the Nineteenth Century* (New York: Praeger, 1973); and Barry A. R. Cooper, "English Solo Keyboard Music of the Middle and Late Baroque," (Ph.D. thesis, Oxford University, 1974). For inventories of Lbl 3, Och 2, and T, see Bruce Gustafson, *French Harpsichord Music of the Seventeenth Century*, Studies in Musicology 11, 3 vols. (Ann Arbor, Mich.: University Microfilms International, 1979). Articles on specific sources follow.

CDp: Malcolm Boyd, "Music Manuscripts in the Mackworth Collection at Cardiff," *Music and Letters* 54 (1973): 133–41.

En: Gwilym Beechey, "A New Source of Seventeenth-Century Keyboard Music," *Music and Letters* 50 (1969): 278–89.

Wc and U: Alexander Silbiger, "Keyboard Music by Corelli's Colleagues: Roman Composers in English Sources," *Nuovissimi Studi Corelliani: Atti del Terzo Congresso Internazionale, Fusignano, 4–7 settembre 1980* (Florence: Leo S. Olschki, 1982), 253–68.

LAuc: Robert Klakowich, "Harpsichord Music by Purcell and Clarke in Los Angeles," *Journal of Musicology* 4 (1985–86): 171–90.

17. London, Royal College of Music, MS 1106. See Brennecke, "Dryden's Odes," 9–10.

18. Hawkins, *General History*, 2:718.

19. Hawkins confused Draghi and Lully with respect to the famous tune from the first act of Lully's *Atys* (1676), known in England as "the Old Cibell." The tune found its way into anthologies printed in England around the turn of the century and even into the opera *The Kingdom of the Birds*, produced at the Haymarket Theatre in 1706. Referring to the opera, Hawkins attributed the tune to "Signor Baptist Draghi" (*General History*, 2:701), possibly influenced by the ascription in *The Second Part of the Division Flute* (1708), which reads "Sigr Baptist." For further details on the Old Cibell, see Thurston Dart, "The Cibell," *Revue belge de musicologie* 6 (1952): 24–30.

20. Transcribed in Dart, ed., *The Second Part of Musick's Hand-maid*, no. 20; and Howard Ferguson, ed., *Early English Keyboard Music* (London: Oxford University Press, 1971), 2:40–43. The piece has even been recorded on disc as a work of Draghi (*Lessons and Ayres*, Trevor Pinnock, harpsichord, CRD Records, CRD 1047). The incipit of this keyboard version is given in the Appendix.

21. Dart, ed., *The Second Part of Musick's Hand-maid*, Additional Notes, no. 20.

22. See Herbert Schneider, *Chronologisch-thematisches Verzeichnis sämtlicher Werke von Jean-Baptiste Lully*, Mainzer Studien zur Musikwissenschaft, vol. 14 (Tutzing: Schneider, 1981), 505. The catalogue does not mention the keyboard versions in *Musick's Hand-maid II* and in Och 2, fol. 11v, nor the single-melody version (for violin?) in London, British Library, MS Add. 17853, fol. 10r. The work may have been composed as one of the *Trios de la chambre du roi*, said by Le Cerf to be among Lully's "premiers Ouvrages" (*Comparaison de la musique italienne et de la musique française* [Brussels, 1705–6; Geneva: Minkoff Reprints, 1972], 2: 144). About the vocal version Le Cerf remarks: "Air fameux d'un de ses divertissemens du petit coucher; & cela malgré la vivacité de la jeunesse & l'apât des paroles Italiennes" (*Comparaison* 2:200). Many airs with Italian words were contained in Lully's ballets and masquerades, though there is no record of "Scocca pur" among them. Consider also the striking similarity of the melody to the Air and Chorus "Les plaisirs ont choisi pour asile" in Act V, scene 2 of *Armide*.

23. Franklin B. Zimmerman, *Henry Purcell 1659–1695: An Analytical Catalogue of his Music* (London: Macmillan, 1963), 395.

24. See entries in Donald Howard Boalch, *Makers of the Harpsichord and Clavichord 1440–1840*, 2d ed. (Oxford: Clarendon Press, 1974), and especially the comment on the Hitchcocks in Frank Hubbard, *Three Centuries of Harpsichord Making* (Cambridge, Mass.: Harvard University Press, 1965), 154.

25. Edward Francis Rimbault, *The Pianoforte . . . with some account of . . . the clavichord, the virginal, the spinet, the harpsichord* (London: R. Cocks and Co., 1860), 68.

26. For example, Thomas Mace described a harpsichord with a variety of stops, all controlled by pedals. Mace, *Musicks Monument* (London, 1676; facs. ed., New York: Broude Brothers, 1966), 235–36. Quoted in Hubbard, *Three Centuries*, 146–47.

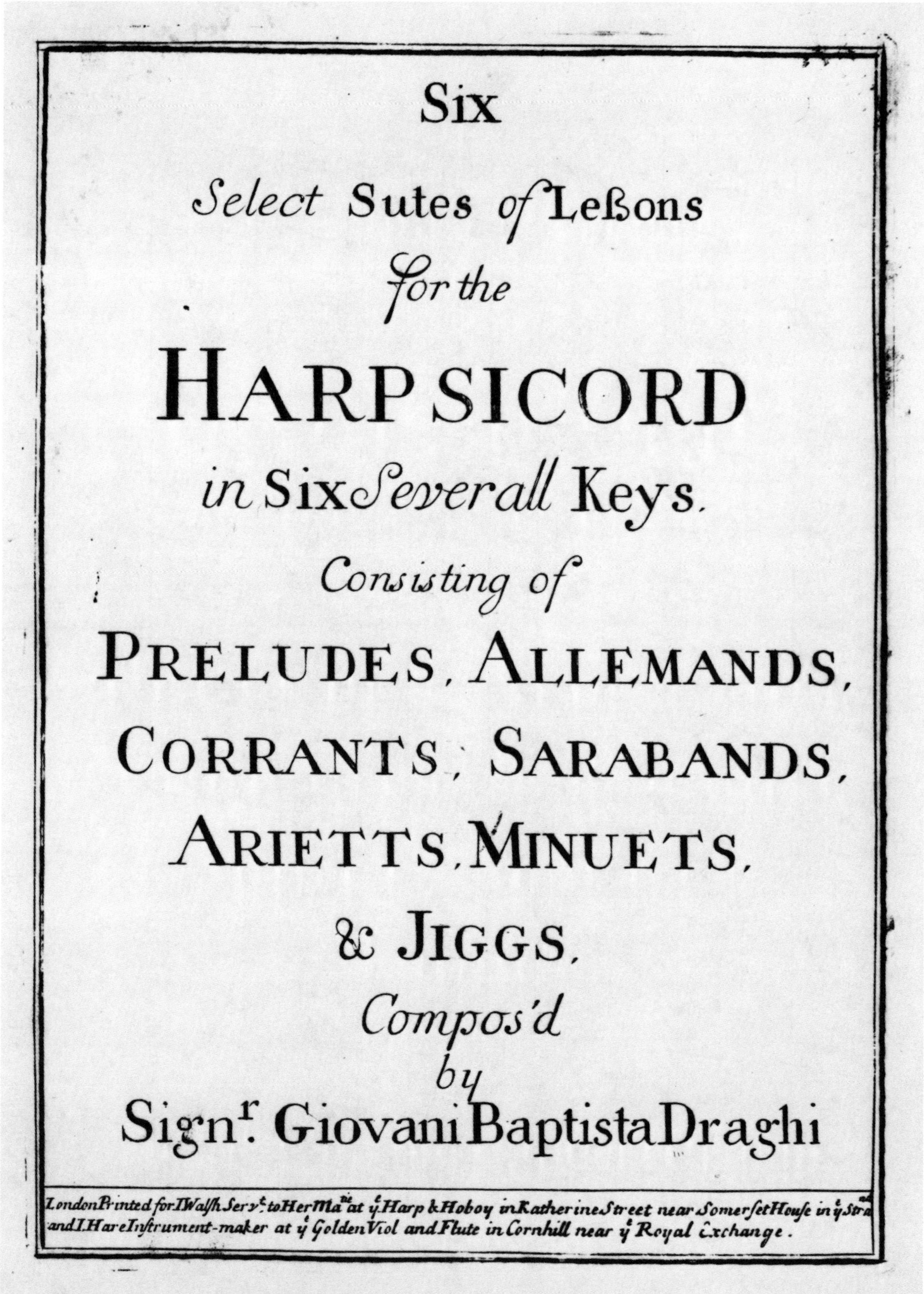

Six

Select Sutes of Leßons

for the

HARPSICORD

in Six Severall Keys.

Consisting of

PRELUDES, ALLEMANDS,
CORRANTS, SARABANDS,
ARIETTS, MINUETS,
& JIGGS,

Compos'd

by

Signᵣ. Giovani Baptista Draghi

London Printed for I. Walsh Serᵛᵗ. to Her Maᵗⁱᵉ at ÿ Harp & Hoboy in Katherine Street near Somerset House in ÿ Strᵃ and I. Hare Instrument-maker at ÿ Golden Viol and Flute in Cornhill near ÿ Royal Exchange.

Plate I. Giovanni Battista Draghi, *Six Select Suites of Lessons for the Harpsichord . . .*
(London: Walsh, [1707]), title page
(Courtesy School of Music Library, Yale University)

Plate II. Giovanni Battista Draghi, first page of Almand ([61] in this edition), Cambridge, Fitzwilliam Museum, Music MS 652, fol. 5v, possible autograph (Courtesy Fitzwilliam Museum)

HARPSICHORD MUSIC

[1] Prelude

[2] Allmand

4

[3] Corrant

[fine]

[4] The Complaint

5

6

[5] Aire

[6] Jigg

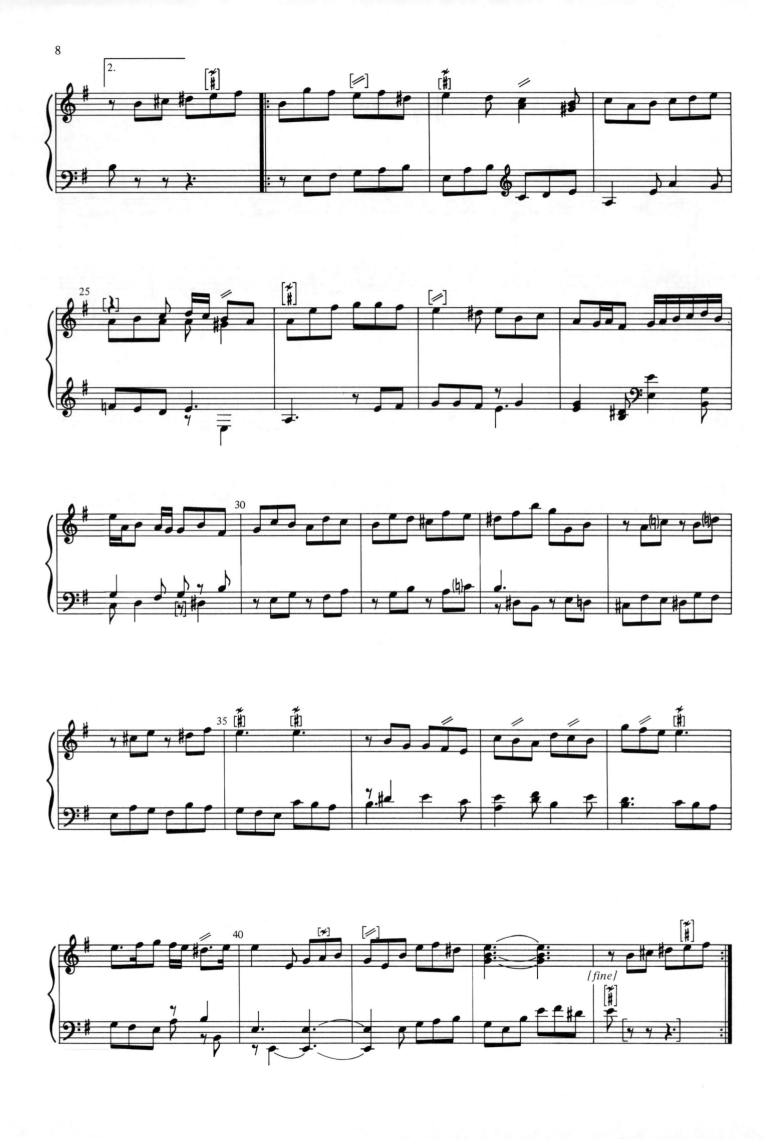

9

[7] Prelude

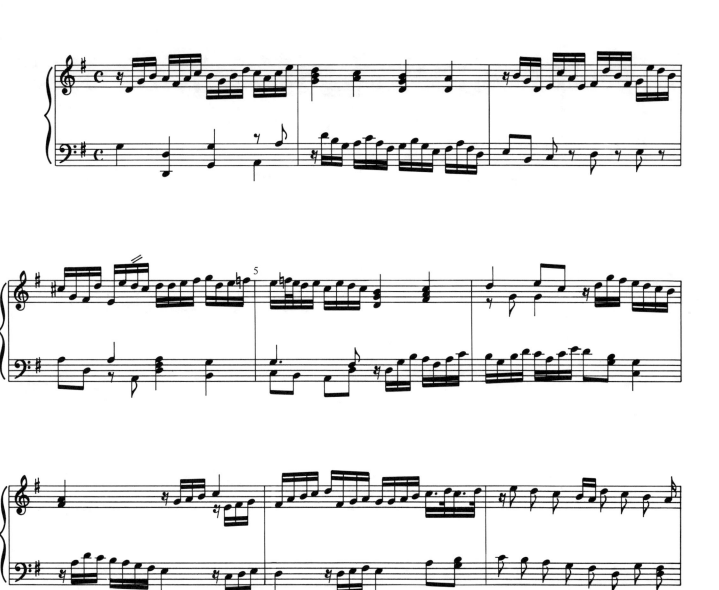

[8] Allmand

[fine]

12

[9] Corrant

[fine]

[10] Saraband

[11] Aire

[12] The Hunting Tune

[13] Prelude

[14] Allmand

[fine]

[15] Corrant

[16] Saraband

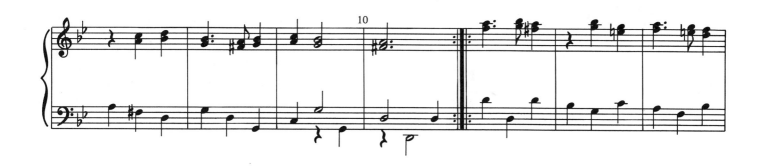

[17] Aire

[18] Jigg

[fine]

[19] Prelude

[20] Allmand

[21] Corrant

[fine]

[22] Saraband

[23] Jigg

[24] Round O

[25] Prelude

29

[26] Allmand

[27] Corrant

[fine]

[28] Saraband

[29] Bore

[fine]

[30] Aire

34

[31] Minuet

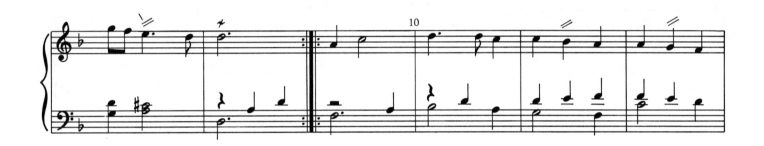

[32] Prelude

[33] Allmand

[34] Aire

[35] Jigg

[36] The Dream

[37] Minuet

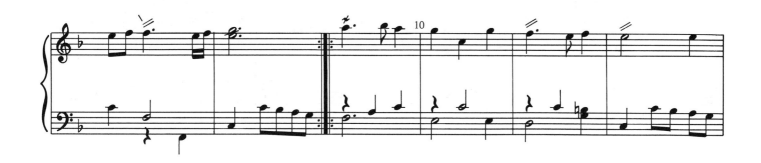

[38] Toccata

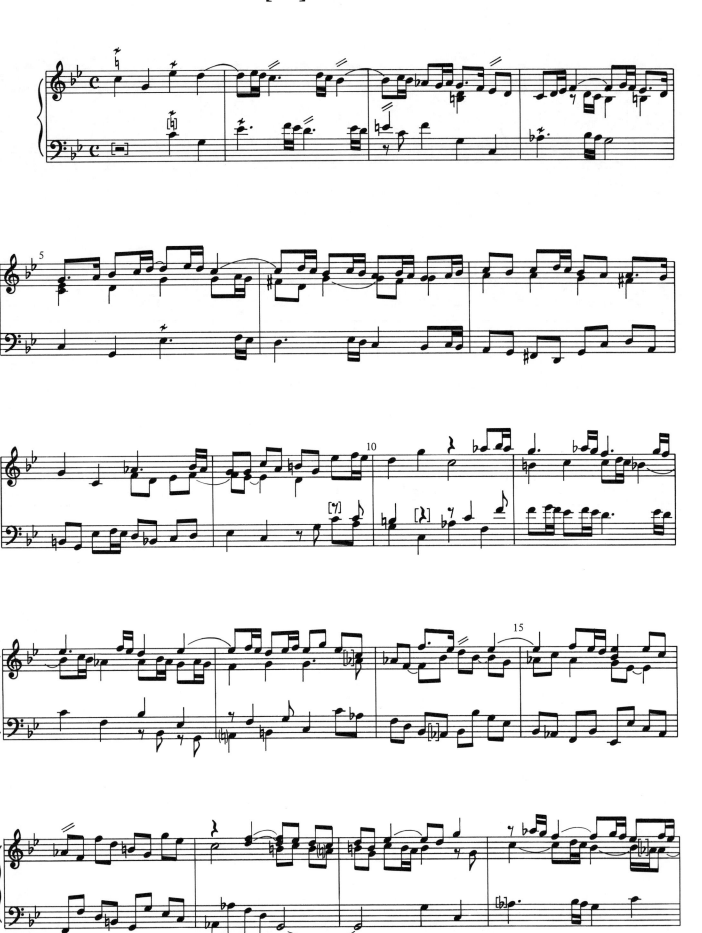

[39] Trumpet

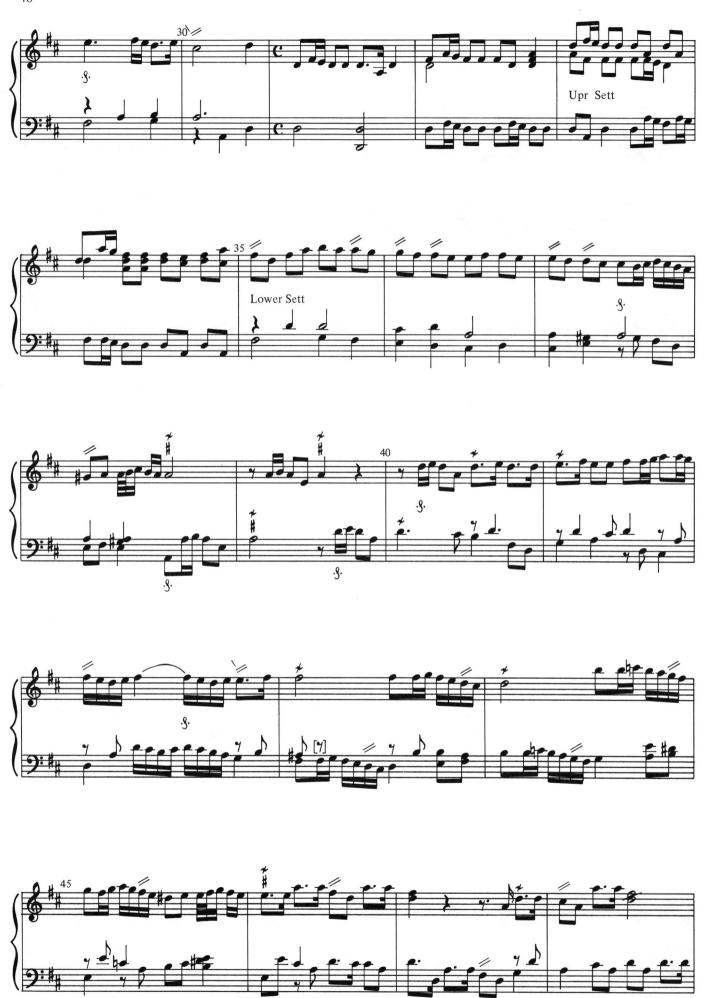

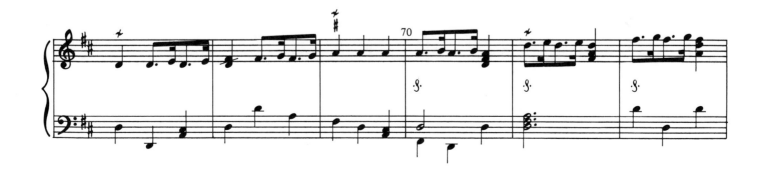

49

slower

[40] Ayre

[41] Prelude

54

[42] Allemande

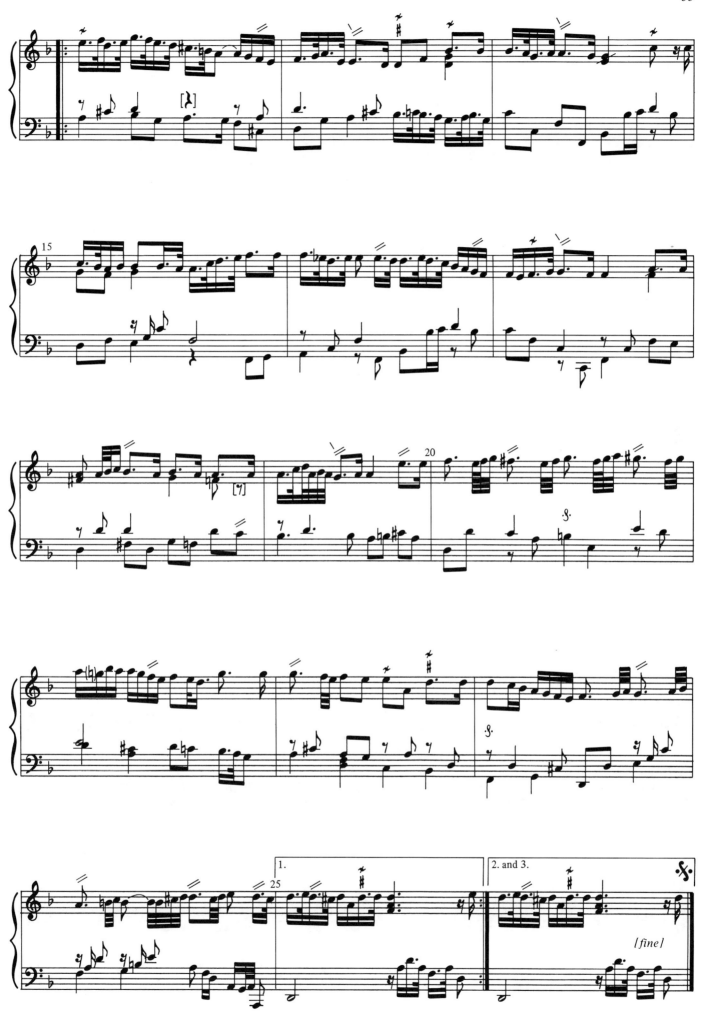

[43] Arieta

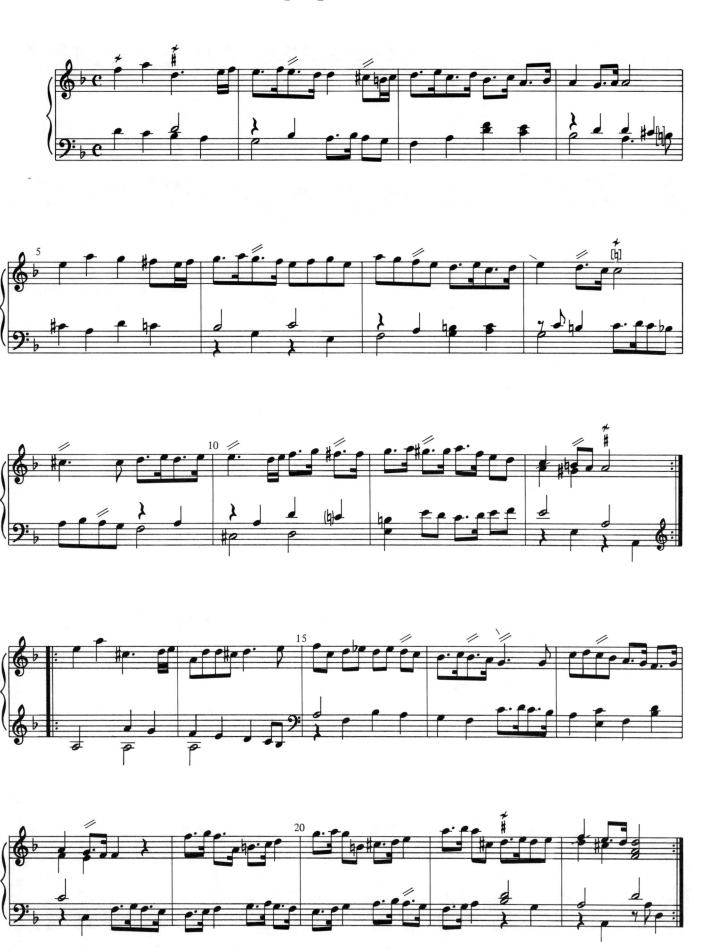

[44] [Bouree]

[fine]

[45] Prelud[e]

60

[46] Alemande

[47] Slow

[48] Roundeaue

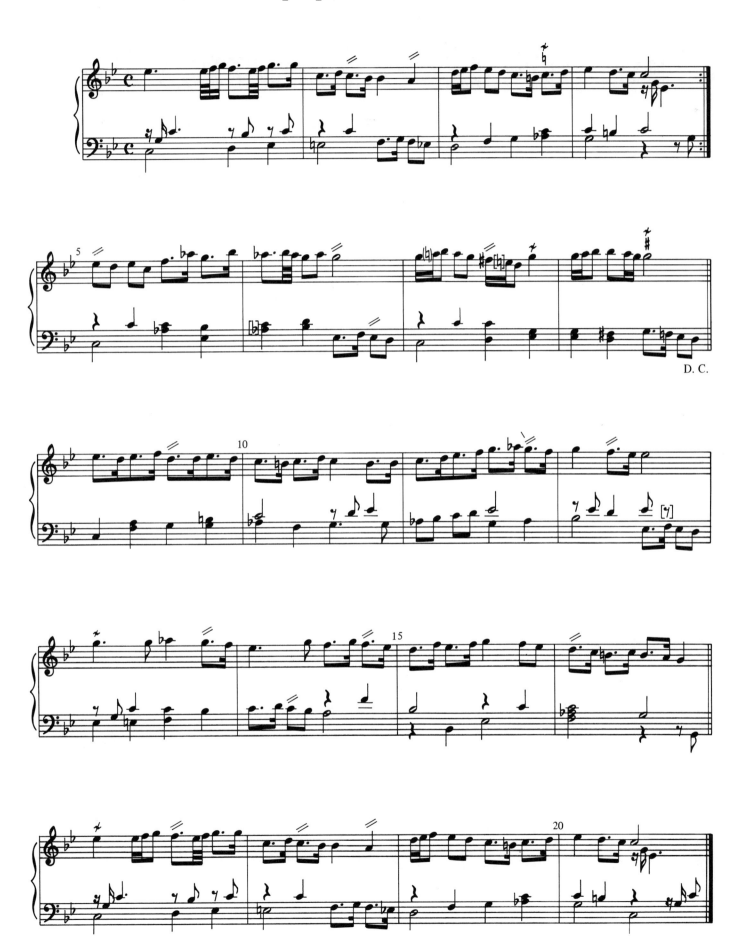

D. C.

[49] Aire

[50] [Aire]

[fine]

[51] [Aire]

[52] [Saraband]

[53] Almond

[54] Prelude

[55] [Allemande]

[56a] Courante

[56b] Double of the Courante

74

[57] [Arietta]

[fine]

[58] Gigue

[fine]

[59] [Aire]

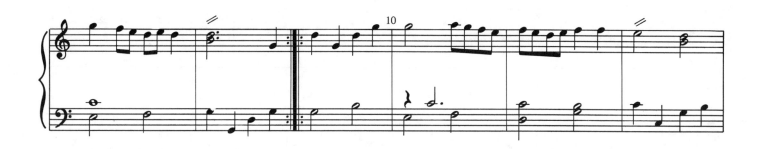

[60] Almond

[fine]

[61] Almand

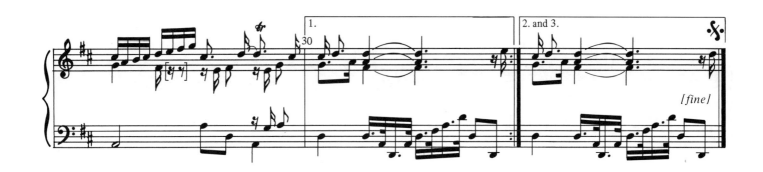

[62] Almaine

[63] Corant

[64] Saraband

[65] [Prelude]

[66] [Allemande]

[67] [Courante]

[68] [Tombeau]

[69] Gigue

[70] Allemande

[71] Rondeau

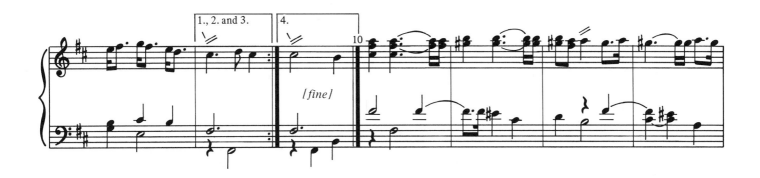

94

[72] [Autre Rondeau]

[73] [Allemande]

[74] Prelude

[75] Almand

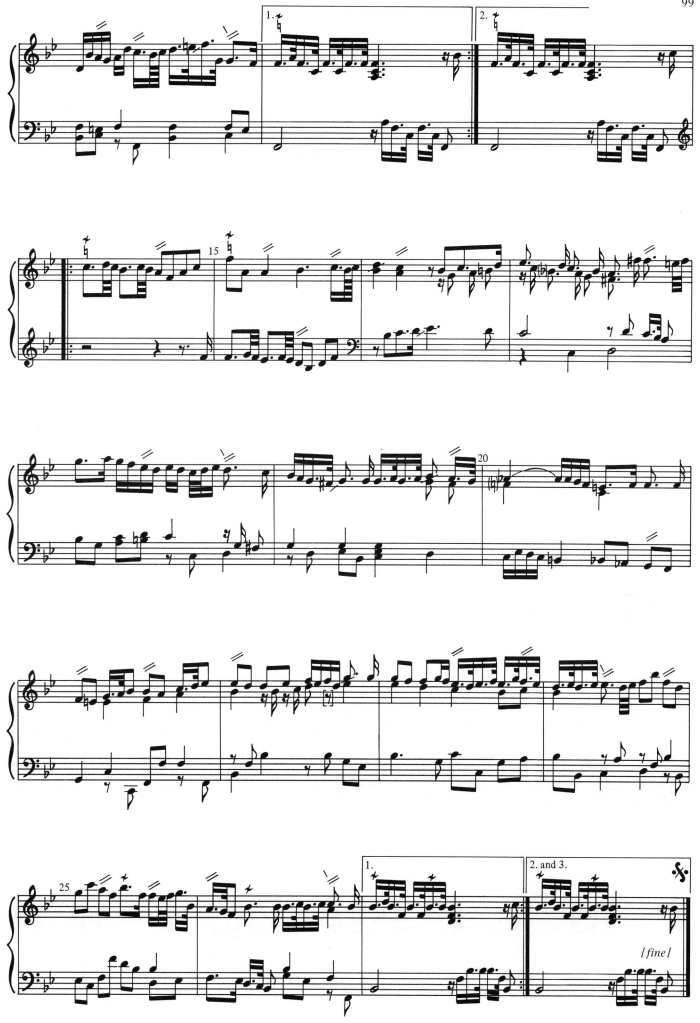

[76] Saraband

[77] [Aire]

[78] [Aire]

[79] Gavotte

[fine]

[80] Slow Minuet

[81] [Almand]

[82] Tune

[83] Tune

108

[84] A Ground

[85] Italian air

Appendix

Ground "Scocca pur"

The C-minor ground from Henry Playford's *Second Part of Musick's Hand-maid* (1689) has long been considered a work of Draghi. As argued in the Preface of this edition (see Authenticity), the "Scocca pur" melody is connected with Lully, and the keyboard version of it (see incipit below) may have been arranged by Purcell.

Lully, LWV 76/3
Keyboard versions
The Second Part of Musick's Hand-maid (1689), no. 20
Och 2, fol. 11v